REINCARNATION

REINCARNATION

REMARKABLE STORIES OF PEOPLE WHO RECALL PAST LIVES

PAUL ROLAND

Capella

This edition published in 2008 by Arcturus Publishing Limited
26/27 Bickels Yard, 151–153 Bermondsey Street,
London SE1 3HA

ISBN: 978-1-84193-912-4

British Library Cataloguing-in-Publication Data: a catalogue record for this book is available from the British Library

Editor: Nigel Matheson
Design: Alex Ingr
Cover design: Peter Ridley

Printed in China

Contents

Dedication

To my editors, Tessa Rose and Nigel Matheson, who have made the task of writing to tight deadlines a pleasure.

Acknowledgements

The author would like to thank Carol Bowman for agreeing to be interviewed and for granting permission to include extracts from her book, *Children's Past Lives* (Bantam), as well as unpublished material from her website: http://www.carolbowman.com.

Thanks also go to Lee Everett-Alkin, for agreeing to be interviewed and for granting permission to include extracts from *Celebrity Regressions* (W. Foulsham), and to Roger Woolger, for giving permission to include extracts from his unpublished work and lectures.

✣ Have You Lived Before? ✣

Birth is not a beginning; death is not an end.

Chuang Tzu

(1) Do you have an obsessive interest in a particular period in history? Do you dream about this time repeatedly and in great detail?
(2) Have you felt drawn to a particular country or location with which you have no obvious connection in this present life?
(3) Do you have a vague sense of having 'lost' something or someone dear to you that you cannot quite recall? Do you feel that there is something 'missing' from your life?
(4) Have you ever felt that you were born 'out of time', that you didn't belong in the present?
(5) Have you ever dreamt that you went back to a strangely familiar place and when you awoke felt unaccountably sad to have returned to the present?
(6) Do you have an uncommonly strong bond with someone outside your family, someone you could call a 'soul mate' whose feelings and opinions are uncannily similar to your own?

(7) Have you ever sensed an inexplicable dislike for someone you have just met without having a reason to distrust them?
(8) Is there a piece of music that transports you to a place or historical period for which you feel a special affinity?
(9) Do you suffer from any chronic conditions for which there is no obvious physical cause?
(10) Do you suffer from a fear or phobia for which there is no logical explanation?
(11) Was there ever a time when you displayed intuitive knowledge of something which you had never been taught or demonstrated a skill that you had never acquired in your present life?
(12) Do you have a talent that you appear to have 'inherited' without having studied or practised that particular discipline?
(13) Have you ever been called 'an old soul'?
(14) Are you more than idly curious to explore your past lives? Do you sense that there is something significant lying just below the surface of your conscious mind waiting to be rediscovered?
(15) Are you burdened by a sense of injustice which cannot be justified by your experiences in your present life?
(16) Are you unaccountably anxious although there is no logical reason for your insecurity?
(17) Do you have a passion for antiques and historical buildings that goes beyond their value and aesthetic beauty?
(18) When you were a child did you ever feel that you had another family somewhere else?
(19) Do you have an uncommonly strong interest in another culture?
(20) When you were a child did you demonstrate abilities, understanding and knowledge in advance of your years?

If you answered 'yes' to **fewer than three** questions, it suggests that you may have *unconsciously suppressed your memories of your past incarnations* because you have been conditioned to deny such ideas as irrational, or you may simply be so preoccupied with the present that you have never given the idea serious thought.

If you answered 'yes' to **between three and five** questions, it indicates that you have *intermittent and involuntary recall of a former life* and that you are ready to make a conscious connection so that these memories can be reawakened at will.

If you answered 'yes' to **six or more** questions, it suggests that you have an *uncommonly strong connection with the Unconscious* and that you have the potential to develop spontaneous recall which can reveal the pattern underlying a string of past lives and the purpose of your present incarnation.

INTRODUCTION

None but very hasty thinkers will reject it on the grounds of inherent absurdity. Like the doctrine of evolution itself, that of transmigration has its roots in the world of reality.

Thomas Huxley, *Evolution and Ethics*

REINCARNATION – the belief that we are all reborn many times in order to experience a succession of lives – is not a New Age fad, but is common to almost every culture on earth. Of the seventy non-Western cultures studied by Dean Shiels, Associate Professor at the University of Wisconsin in the late 1970s, an astonishing ninety-five per cent shared a belief in the transmigration of souls. This belief in the immortality of the human soul shaped the lives of our ancestors, whose culture and customs were determined by their expectations of reward and punishment in the world beyond.

Rationalists and materialists argue that when we die we simply cease to be: they maintain that life, consciousness and self-awareness are extinguished as swiftly as the snuffing out of a candle flame. But if that is so, why is our belief in life after death so universal and unshakable? And how do we explain the fact that reincarnation remains the cornerstone of the world's oldest religions, philosophies and faiths, including Buddhism, Hinduism, Judaism and early Christianity (though it was later declared heretical by the Church for reasons revealed in this book)?

It is estimated that as many as fifty million people (sixty per cent of the world's population) believe in reincarnation (source: Dr J. Chiappalone, author of *Keys to Reality*) and though the vast majority are of Eastern origin and do so because it is a central tenet of their religion, an increasing number of Westerners are beginning to accept this idea.

Part of the reason for this steady increase in the belief in reincarnation stems from a growing interest in other spiritual traditions and the acceptance of esoteric teachings which began when the Beatles and their guru, Maharishi Mahesh Yogi, introduced Transcendental Meditation and Eastern ideas to the West in the late 1960s.

More recently there has been an intensification of interest in psychic phenomena and the paranormal as evidenced by the popularity of fictional

In the West, interest in the esoteric has grown since the teachings of Maharishi Mahesh Yogi became popular in the 1960s

TV series such as *Medium* and a string of psychic reality programmes such as *Britain's Most Haunted* and *The Antiques Ghost Show* and the globally-syndicated US shows *Crossing Over* and *Beyond.* The two last-named items star the real-life mediums John Edward and James Van Praagh whose studio séances have produced credible evidence of survival after death and brought the subject into the living rooms of people who would never have considered consulting a professional psychic.

A recent opinion poll revealed that a staggering seventy per cent of the adult population of the US now believe in the survival of the soul after death (source: Harris Poll, 2005), and that one in four people accept the possibility that they have lived before. Statistical surveys are, of course, notoriously unreliable for a number of reasons, the main one being that they fail to take account of those who choose not to respond. When the subject of the survey is as personal as one's spiritual beliefs, it is likely that the majority of those who choose to abstain are the very people who could tip the balance in favour of a positive result.

So is there any hard physical evidence to justify the widely-held belief that our present life is just one in a series of incarnations, or is the concept of reincarnation merely wishful thinking on the part of those who need to believe that they led a far more interesting life last time around? After all, how many of us are really likely to have been bona fide historical celebrities? When considering the validity of such claims one has to consider the motive of the person making the claim. But even though some individuals may simply be seeking attention, or unwittingly deceiving themselves, that does not necessarily invalidate the techniques used to recover these 'memories', nor the 'memories' themselves.

The aim of this book is to present the wealth of compelling evidence offered by those who have undergone hypnotic regression, as well as that provided by the countless incidents of Near Death Experiences (NDEs), which appear to prove the existence of the human soul. If the etheric or astral body is our natural state of being, our true nature, then reincarnation

can be seen as simply a natural stage in the lifecycle of the human spirit and not as a supernatural phenomenon.

True luxury is being able to find the time to sit and think about who we really are, where we have come from and where we are heading

NDEs involve individuals leaving their bodies, travelling through a tunnel and emerging in a new world of light and colour to be reunited with their loved ones on the other side of life. Even those of contrasting backgrounds and beliefs describe a strikingly similar core experience which suggests that this phenomenon is not a delusion of the dying brain as the sceptics contend. Such incidents are frequently triggered by a physical crisis such as a violent accident, a serious illness, extreme exhaustion or the influence of an anaesthetic when the connection between the etheric, or astral, body and the physical shell is at its weakest. But this temporary separation of spirit and body can also be induced at will during states of deep relaxation and can occur spontaneously in certain stages of sleep.

A Gallup poll in 1992 suggested that as many as thirteen million Americans believed that they had had an Out Of Body Experience (OBE), but again the very nature of an OBE is likely to dissuade many people from sharing this most profoundly personal experience with strangers. Some are even reluctant to confide in their families for fear of being ridiculed, while I have personally known several people who have dismissed their own experience as a lucid dream because it contradicted their religious beliefs. For this reason it can be assumed that the many tens of thousands of OBEs

NDEs are common across many different cultures. Individuals leave their bodies and travel to a new world of light and colour

and NDEs that are to be found in the countless books on the subject, and which are posted on numerous websites around the world, are only a tiny fraction of those stories that could be told.

Recent breakthroughs in medical science appear to offer incontrovertible proof that NDEs are a fact of life. And if such episodes are as common as the research suggests, are we now closer than ever to discovering the mysteries of life, death and rebirth?

Yet for many people their belief in a life after death is not based on a profound personal experience. Instead, it stems from their reluctance to imagine a moment when they might cease to exist. Also, many of those who can imagine an afterlife find it too incredible to accept the premise that they could be reborn in a new body – particularly if it will involve incarnating as the opposite sex. People who find difficulty in remembering what they did last week are naturally sceptical when they are faced with those who claim to be able to recall their previous lives in infinite detail. They point out that recent studies that question the validity of hypnotic regression have shown that we are capable of deceiving ourselves by dredging up long-forgotten images and impressions from the unconscious, suggesting that many past life recollections may have a more mundane explanation.

But what other theories can explain the extraordinary claims made by children who insist that they have recognized their relatives from an earlier life and can identify long-dead family members from photographs which they have never seen before? How else can one explain the sisters who remember how they 'died', the strangers who shared the same dreams and the little Indian girl who walked blindfolded through a town she had never visited in her present incarnation, then led investigators to her former home where she recovered the personal possessions she had hidden there in a previous incarnation?

In the following pages you will find dozens of similar stories of people who can recall their previous incarnations in incredible detail, including those who were born with birthmarks in the shape of fatal wounds sustained in an earlier incarnation, the soul mates working through 'unfinished business' from previous lives and the celebrities who are left wondering if their talents were inherited from an earlier incarnation.

> *The virtues we acquire, which develop slowly within us, are the invisible links that bind each one of our existences to the others – existences which the spirit alone remembers, for matter has no memory for spiritual things. The endless legacy of the past to the present is the secret source of human genius.*
>
> Honoré de Balzac

'Many of those who can imagine an afterlife find it too incredible to accept the premise they could be reborn in a new body'

I

From Prehistory to Christianity

Civilizations and Religions from Prehistory Onwards

Death and life are not far apart. When I look for their origin it goes back into infinity; when I look for their end, it proceeds without termination. Life is the follower of death and death is the predecessor of life. What we can point to are the faggots that have been consumed: but the fire is transmitted elsewhere.

Chuang Tzu

THERE is strong physical evidence that mankind's belief in reincarnation may predate recorded history. More than 12,000 years ago it was common practice for Stone Age tribes to bury their dead in the foetal position, together with their personal possessions, in anticipation of their physical rebirth in the next world.

Even before the founding of the earliest civilizations, so-called 'primitive' peoples in remote regions of Africa, Asia, Australia and the Americas acknowledged the cycle of death and rebirth in their art, rituals and customs. This found expression in the cult of animism, the idea that all forms of life, from plants to human beings, are animated by a universal life force. This belief became more formalized with the establishment of the first civilizations in Mesopotamia and ancient Egypt (*c.*3,300BC).

✣ THREE SOULS ✣

ASTRAL PROJECTION, or soul travel, is still practised by the shaman of tribal societies as far apart as Africa, Australasia, North and South America and the Arctic. Through a combination of ritual drumming, dancing, chanting, fasting and natural narcotics they induce a state of ecstasy (meaning 'to stand outside') which creates a separation of mind and body so that they can contact their animal spirit guides and their ancestors to ask for healing or guidance.

A shaman in Mexico City uses time-honoured techniques to induce ecstasy

Similarly, in Tibet, China and India initiates of the esoteric disciplines were required to prove they had mastered the ability to project the astral body at will during meditation. The ancient Chinese possessed a manual called *The Secret of the Golden Flower,* which described a sequence of breathing exercises, yogic-styled postures and contemplation guaranteed to liberate the spirit body (the *thankhi*) through the 'pineal door', which was believed to be located in the centre of the forehead.

This belief that the soul can be released through the 'Third Eye', the centre of psychic sight between the brows, is the origin of the cobra-shaped headpiece with which every Egyptian pharaoh was crowned and it remains a sacred symbol today. It is exemplified in the dot which every Hindu female wears on her forehead.

It is highly significant that no fewer than 57 cultures – as diverse as the Inuit of Alaska, certain Native American tribes, the Burmese and the Zulu in Africa – share the idea of there being a spirit double. In *The Soul of a People* (MacMillan, 1905), author H. Fielding Hall notes that this belief is so strong among the Burmese people, and so embedded in their culture, that they defy their monks, who deny the concept of reincarnation themselves.

> *When a man dies, his soul remains, his 'I' has only changed its habitation... many can remember something of these former lives of theirs... of course, it is clearer to some than to others... when the day's work is over [they share] stories of second birth... Many children, the Burmese will tell you, remember their former lives. As they grow older the memories die away and they forget, but to the young children they are very clear... This [then] is the common belief of the people... A man has a soul, and it passes from life to life, as a traveller from inn to inn, till at length it is ended in heaven. But not till he has attained heaven in his heart will he attain heaven in reality.*

The Third Eye is a symbol of enlightenment. It is said to be the gateway to the realms within and to higher consciousness

Writing about the Zulu tradition in *Reincarnation: A New Horizon in Science, Religion and Society*, (Julian Press, New York, 1984), Sylvia Cranston and Carey Williams recorded the belief that:

> *Within the body is a soul: within the soul is a spark of Itango, the universal spirit. After the death of the body, Idhozi (the soul) hovers for a while near the body and then departs to Esilweni, the place of the beasts. In Esilweni the soul assumes a shape part beast, part human, before it rises... According to the strength of the animal nature, the soul throws aside its beast-like shape and moves onward to a place of rest. There it sleeps, till a time comes when it dreams that something to do and learn awaits it on earth; then it awakes and returns to earth and is born again as a child. The soul repeats this until it becomes one with the Itongo.*

Belief in a spirit double or 'dream body' is the basis of the Roman *larva*, the Tibetan *delok*, the German *Doppelgänger*, the English *fetch*, the Norwegian *vardger* and the Scottish *taslach*. Even the Vikings, a people not commonly considered to be spiritual, preserved the idea in their mythology. In the *Poetic Edda*, Helgi Hjorvarosson and his Valkyrie mistress Svafa are reborn as Helgi Hundingsbane and Sigrún and in a subsequent life as Helgi Haddingjaskati and Kara.

Sigrun was early dead of sorrow and grief. It was believed in olden times that people were born again, but that is now called old wives' folly. Of Helgi and Sigrun it is said that they were born again; he became Helgi Haddingjaskati, and she Kara the daughter of Halfdan, as is told in the Lay of Kara, and she was a Valkyrie.

The Druids, pagan priests of the British Isles, also believed in reincarnation. Julius Caesar attributed the stubbornness of the Celts to their belief in the cycle of death and rebirth.

They wish to inculcate this as one of their leading tenets, that souls do not become extinct, but pass after death from one body to another, and they think that men by this tenet are in a great degree stimulated to valour, the fear of death being disregarded.

Above: Valkyries carried off the bravest slain in battle to Valhalla. Right: Druids prepare the ranks of the Celts for battle with Rome

More remarkable is the fact that many of the world's spiritual traditions acknowledge the existence of not two but three components to the human spirit. The Greeks spoke of the the *psyche*, the *pneuma* and the *nous*; the Muslims acknowledged the *sirr*, the *ruh* and the *nafs*; the Hindus talked of the *atman*, the *jiva* and the *pranamayakosha*; while the Jewish mystics contemplated the existence of the *neshamah*, the *ruah* and the *nefash*, which the Christians assimilated and externalized in the concept of the Holy Trinity – the Father, Son and Holy Ghost – which was misinterpreted as referring to external entities.

Surely this cannot be mere coincidence. Such universally accepted concepts can only come from a shared experience.

As Harvard Professor Dr Carol Zaleski has

observed, 'A conviction that life surpasses death, however intensely felt, will eventually lose its vitality and become a mere fossil record, as alien as any borrowed doctrine, unless it is tested and rediscovered in daily life.'

✣ MESOPOTAMIA ✣

THE SUMERIANS of Mesopotamia were accomplished astrologers and mathematicians, who also believed that they shared the earth with the gods who walked among them in human form. Consequently their concept of the afterlife was limited to an acknowledgement of the existence of the human soul, which they imagined was dispersed into the wind like a wisp of dust a year after the death of the body: it having been deprived of the vital force which sustained it in life.

Vision of Hell: Dante is led by his spiritual guide Virgil past a sinner who is buried in an open tomb for eternity in The Divine Comedy

Their conquerors, the Babylonians (*c*.1790BC) and later the Assyrians (*c*.1100BC) held that their gods were embodied in the land, the sea and the stars as well as personifying abstract concepts such as Fate. This led to the necessity to create a whole pantheon of gods each of whom presided over his own paradise. Those who honoured their chosen deity by displaying courage in battle would be guaranteed a place at their feet, a belief which gave rise to the cult of hero worship. However, those who displeased the gods would be imprisoned in the underworld, deep in the earth in a place that is clearly a forerunner of the Greek concept of Hades and the Christian Hell. The forsaken souls lived in perpetual darkness and were tormented by hunger and thirst, rising only at night to wander the streets while scavenging for discarded scraps. In the seventh tablet of Gilgames this place of torment is known variously as the Land of No Return and the House of Gloom.

Upon the house whose entrance hath no exit,
Upon the path whose way hath no return,
Upon the house whose enterers are deprived of light,
Where dust is their nourishment, their food mud,
Light they see not, in darkness they dwell...

By contrast, the fortunate souls who were permitted to dwell with the gods in the heavens enjoyed the companionship of their loved ones who had passed over before them and were sustained by drinking the purest water from an endless stream.

It is significant that the Sumerians and their successors in this region made a distinction between the immortal soul (which they called *utukka*) and the spirit (*edimmu*), which can be thought of as the residual personal energy left behind on the physical plane like a fading echo of the parting soul.

This distinction between layers of the spirit found its ultimate expression in the ancient Egyptian cult of the dead.

The bodies of the Ancient Egyptians were embalmed and then wrapped in linen to prepare them for eternal life. Death was not so much feared as celebrated

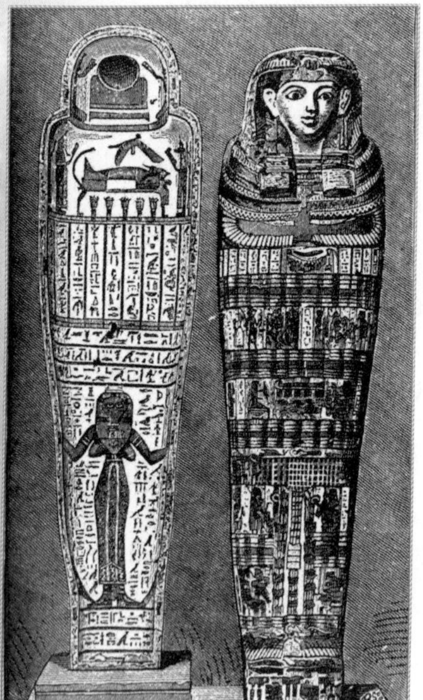

✣ EGYPT: THE CULT OF THE DEAD ✣

... the Egyptians were the first to teach that the human soul is immortal, and at the death of the body enters into some other living thing then coming to birth; and after passing through all creatures, of land, sea, and air (which cycle it completes in three thousand years) it enters once more into a human body at birth. Some of the Greeks, early and late, have used this doctrine as if it were their own...

Herodotus (Bk. II, Sec. 123)

THE EGYPTIAN custom of placing a mummified corpse into a series of sarcophagi of increasing refinement symbolized the three elements of the human spirit – the *ka*, *ba* and *akh* – which equate with the astral body, the mind and the immortal soul. According to esoteric tradition the astral body is the matrix of plastic etheric energy which is a ghostly double of our physical form. It is the disembodied self which can become detached during an out-of-body experience and which is secured to the physical by an umbilical cord that is only severed upon death.

> *The soul passes from form to form; and the mansions of her pilgrimage are manifold. Thou puttest off thy bodies as raiment; and as vesture dost thou fold them up. Thou art from old, oh soul of man, yea thou art from everlasting.*
>
> *Egyptian Hermetic Fragment*

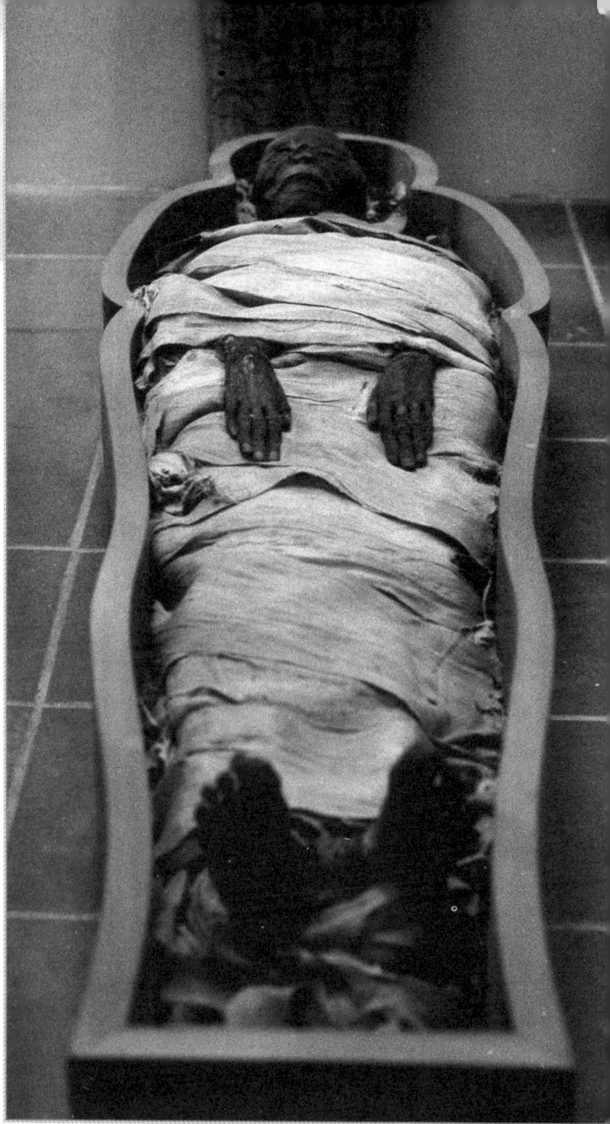

It seems likely that the elaborate Egyptian funeral rites intended to guide the disembodied soul through the underworld were grounded in first hand knowledge of the spirit realm obtained by their high priests during initiation ceremonies conducted in the pyramids. Although built primarily as tombs for the pharaohs, the pyramids may have served a secondary purpose as a sacred space where the high priests would perform magical rites, 'assuming the god form' of the deity with whom they wished to communicate in the expectation of stimulating an astral journey into the upper realms. Once separated from the confines of their physical body they would be free to explore the universe and commune with the gods. The three pyramids at Giza have been shown to be in alignment with three stars in the constellation of Orion in the Milky Way. Orion held a mystical significance for the Egyptians who believed that it was the realm of Osiris, ruler of the underworld and judge of the dead.

Before they were consigned to the afterlife, mummies had their mouths prised open by a priest to admit sustenance and to renew the five senses

The shape of the pyramids was designed to focus the earth's magnetic energies to such a degree that the initiate would be unable to resist the force that was drawing their astral self out of their body. This theory was tested in the 1930s by the intrepid English occultist Dr Paul Brunton, who was granted permission to conduct his unique experiment in the King's Chamber of the Great Pyramid. There he experienced an involuntary astral excursion.

... all my muscles became taut, after which a paralysing lethargy began to creep over my limbs. My entire body became heavy and numb... I felt myself sinking inwards in consciousness to some central point within my brain... I had the sensation of being caught up in a tropical whirlwind and seemed to pass upwards through a narrow hole; then there was the momentary dread of being launched into infinite space... I had gone ghost-like out of my earthly body.

Pyramid Power

SOME YEARS AGO a group of American scientists considered the possibility that the shape and dimensions of the pyramid structure itself with its four triangular sides and square base might generate a heightened energy field in the same way that a dowsing rod or pendulum is thought to focus the earth's magnetic energy through the 'medium' of the diviner. Nothing conclusive could be proven but modern day visitors to Egypt often report feeling a warm tingling sensation while touring the tombs and this may be what is commonly referred to as 'pyramid power', which is said by some to generate certain phenomena such as sharpening blunt razor blades when they are left overnight in a model pyramid.

When the well-known British psychic Tony Stockwell visited the Great Pyramid some years ago he couldn't resist the temptation to touch the walls of the Grand Gallery despite the watchful eye of the guard and the notices warning visitors to refrain from doing so.

'At the very instant my hands touched the wall, I felt this great surge of white light and energy cascade through my body,' he recalled in his autobiography, *Spirited*. 'It was as if I had plugged my body into a major power source... For weeks afterwards, I was lit up, on cloud nine. I felt renewed, energized, healed of all weariness.'

✤ GREECE: THE PHILOSOPHERS ✤

The soul, still a dragged captive, will tell of all the man did and felt; but upon death there will appear, as time passes, memories of the lives lived before, some of the events of the most recent life being dismissed as trivial. As it grows away from the body, it will revive things forgotten in the corporeal state. And if it passes in and out of one body after another, it will tell over the events of the discarded life. It will treat as present that which it has just left, and it will remember much from the former existence. But with lapse of time it will come to forgetfulness of many things that were mere accretion.

Plotinus

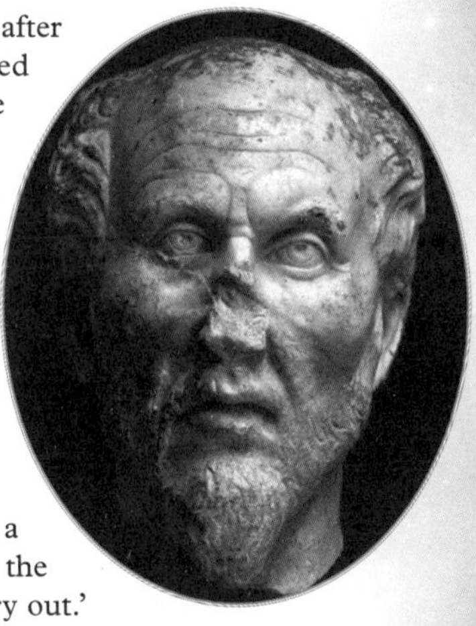

THE ANCIENT Greeks took the question of life after death very seriously. Their greatest thinkers named themselves philosophers (meaning 'those who are concerned with what is under the ground') in acknowledgement of their determination to solve the question which science could never hope to answer.

Pythagoras, the sixth century BC Greek mystic and mathematician, boasted that he had lived many lives, including that of a warrior at the siege of Troy, a prophet, a peasant, a merchant and a harlot, although it is not known by what means he glimpsed these scenes of a former life. He may have seen them in meditation or been told of them by an oracle. Once, he put his philosophy into practice, intervening to prevent a man from beating a dog saying: 'Do not hit him, it is the soul of a friend of mine. I recognized when I heard it cry out.'

But perhaps the greatest among the great minds of ancient Greece was Plato (*c*.427–347BC) who defined the margins of debate within philosophy and of whom it has been said that all subsequent philosophy has been a mere footnote. His teachings dominated that of the Athenian mystery schools which flourished for 900 years after his death, central to which was the concept of reincarnation. It is thought that Plato had adopted the teachings of his mentor Pherecydes, an initiate of the Orphic mysteries, whose followers taught that the soul is literally imprisoned by the body until it is freed by death, whereupon it is confined in another body until set free by the gods once it has attained a degree of purification and self-knowledge. The key to this enlightened state of being was encapsulated in the motto inscribed over the entrance to the Oracle at Delphi: 'Know Thyself'. And it remains the maxim of all those who would seek

the answers to the mysteries of life and death to this day.

Plato openly professed his belief in reincarnation and described how the soul might attain perfection through a process of purification or rebirths. Describing the process in the *Phaedrus,* he stated that the lowest of the nine ranks of human beings were born as tyrants and thieves while those who lived righteous lives gradually ascended to the higher levels of increasing virtuousness. At the fourth level the soul may be reborn in the body of an athlete or physician whereas the third rank includes politicians and academics; above these levels would be found righteous rulers and warriors. Finally, the enlightened soul may be reborn into the body of a philosopher, an artist or an aesthete before returning upon death to the Elysian fields of eternal bliss (below).

Pythagoras boasted about past lives though he left no writings on how he learnt about these

In the mythical story of Er, which ends the *Republic*, Plato preserved one of the earliest written accounts of a Near Death Experience (NDE) in Western literature. His eponymous hero was a soldier whose death in battle presaged his journey through the underworld. Twelve days after his death Er returns to life and recounts his experiences of the underworld where he witnesses the disembodied souls of the deceased returning from heaven and from purgatory to choose their new lives on Earth, some as humans and some as animals. The Greek doctrine of rebirth, known as 'metempsychosis', occurs in many Platonic dialogues such as *Phaedrus, Meno, Phaedo, Timaeus* and *Laws. Meno* is of particular importance because it preserves a discourse on the nature of the soul by Plato's teacher, Socrates (469–399BC) who observed that 'all enquiry and all learning is but recollection'.

In the first century AD Plutarch presented what he insisted was a true account of a NDE. The subject of his tale, Aridaeus of Asia Minor, left his body after receiving a blow on the head and while wandering confused in the darkness between the worlds met the spirit of his uncle who reassured Aridaeus that he was not dead and should return to his body while he was still able to re-enter it. In the course of the story Plutarch mentions the 'silver cord' which binds Aridaeus to the physical plane, a detail which is frequently mentioned in modern tales of NDEs.

> *Your soul's cable is stretched down to your body, to which it is anchored, and allows no further upward slack or play… We know that the soul is indestructible and should think of its experience as like that of a bird in a cage. If it has been kept in a body for a long time and become tamed to this life as a result of all sorts of involvements and long habituation, it will alight back to a body again after birth and will never stop becoming entangled in the passions and chances of this world.*

The Greeks, in turn, strongly influenced Roman intellectuals such as Ennius, Persius, Lucretius and Horace who referred to the soul as 'the genius': which gave rise to the idea that a person who is in direct communication with his Higher or True Self is an exceptional and inspired individual, a genius. Incidentally, the Greek word for the soul was *daemon* which was later corrupted

For Plutarch, the soul's imprisonment in the body is akin to a bird that is trapped in its cage, and lengthy captivity inevitably leads to many woes

'For many millions, rebirth is as certain as the rising of the morning sun and as natural as the cycle of the seasons'

by the early Church, who used the term to denote an evil spirit, the idea being that anyone who believed themselves to be divine must be possessed by madness or a malevolent spirit.

> *Perfect justice rules the world for the Powers that are superior to us know the whole life of the Soul and all its former lives.*
>
> *Iamblichus*

✣ IN THE EAST ✣

The end of birth is death; the end of death is birth.

Bhagavad Gita (Chapter 2)

REINCARNATION is a fact of life for the many millions who adhere to the religions and philosophies of the East. For them rebirth is as certain as the rising of the morning sun and as natural as the cycle of the seasons. It is the one eternal truth around which debate on the meaning of life and the nature of the self can revolve, but within the various traditions and schools there is considerable disagreement as to the nature of the spirit or self which returns to earth.

The Hindu sacred texts known as the Upanishads in which the concept of reincarnation was first recorded *c.*800BC, envisages each human soul as a distinct entity, a grain of salt in the vast ocean of the universe (salt being a precious mineral in India and therefore highly symbolic).

> *All the diverse elements, in the end, go back to the source and are absorbed in it, as all waters are finally absorbed in the ocean… A lump of salt may be produced by separating it from the water of the ocean. But when it is dropped into the ocean, it becomes one with the ocean and cannot be separated again.*

Some have interpreted this to mean that each individual human personality is indistinguishable from the mass and that each human being exists merely to serve the greater good, but another passage from these most ancient scriptures suggests that each human life is precious because every one is animated by a spark of Brahman, the universal spirit.

> *The Self… does not die when the body dies. Concealed in the heart of all*

beings lies the 'atma', the Spirit, the Self; smaller than the smallest atom, greater than the greatest spaces.

Katha Upanishad

In the end, all the diverse elements go back to the source and are absorbed in it, as all waters are finally absorbed in the ocean

Death is nothing more than the casting-off of clothes we have outgrown. Like the butterfly emerging from the cocoon, or the snake that sheds its skin, we discard the physical shell and return to our true form in the world of spirit.

Worn-out garments
Are shed by the body:
Worn-out bodies
Are shed by the dweller
Within the body.
New bodies are donned
By the dweller, like garments.

Bhagavad Gita (Chapter 2)

Death is nothing more than the casting-off of clothes that we have outgrown. It's like the butterfly emerging from the cocoon...

And again,

> *The embodied one within the body of everyone, Bharata, is ever undestroyable. Therefore you should not grieve for any being... [It is] as when one layeth his worn-out robes away... taking new ones, sayeth, 'These will I wear to-day!' So putteth by the spirit lightly its garb of flesh, and passeth to inherit a residence afresh.*
>
> *Bhagavad Gita (Chapter 2)*

According to both Hindu and Buddhist teachings, desire rather than experience is the dynamic which ensures our return to earth, despite the suffering we must endure here. In our search for fulfilment we turn away from the spiritual path for which we need patience and self-discipline and instead seek a quick fix by gratifying our senses. This hunger to experience life draws us back into another body again and again until we realize that we can only satiate our desires but never satisfy them, for we are living in a world of illusion, a world where everything we crave has no lasting value. Everything in this material world that seems so real is impermanent and in trying to keep it from running through our hands we forget what is really important – the fulfilment of our purpose on earth and the realization of our true nature. It is only when we have finally overcome this addiction to the pleasures and diversions that the world has to offer that we will break free of the wheel of death and rebirth and be reunited with the source.

> *The individual self, augmented by its aspirations, sense contact, visual impressions and delusion, assumes successive forms in accordance with its actions... So it is that we live in accordance with our deep, driving desire. It is this desire at the time of death that determines what our next life is to be. We will come back to Earth to work out the satisfaction of that desire.*
>
> *Svetasvtara Upanishad*

In the *Brihadaranyaka Upanishad* the sage Yajnavalkya reveals to King Janaka that death is not a new state of being but merely an extension of the sleeping state when the soul and the body are temporarily disconnected.

Leaving the bodily world through the door of dream, the sleepless spirit views the sleeping powers... soaring upward and downward in dreamland

> *What is the soul? It is the consciousness in the life powers. It is the light within the heart... The Spirit of man has two dwelling places: both this world and the other world. The borderland between them is the third, yet it remains unchanged. Leaving the bodily world through the door of dream, the sleepless spirit views the sleeping powers... soaring upward and downward in dreamland, the god makes manifold forms; now laughing and rejoicing with fair beauties, now beholding terrible things... then clothed in radiance, returns to his home, [he] the gold gleaming genius, swan of everlasting. [From this state, called sushupti, when the body is in deepest slumber and the soul is said to be completely free] the spirit of man returns again by the same path hurrying back to his former dwelling place in the world of waking...*

The loss of a loved one should not be mourned, therefore, for separation is an illusion.

The wise in heart mourn not for those that live, nor those that die. Never the spirit was born; the spirit shall cease to be never. Never was time it was not. End are beginning are dreams! Death hath not touched it at all, dead though the house of it seems! Nay, as when one layeth his worn out robes away, and, taking new ones sayeth, 'These will I wear today!' So putteth by the spirit lightly its garb of flesh, and passeth to inherit a residence afresh.

Bhagavad Gita (Chapter 2)

Buddhism

To be born there and to die there, to die there and to be born elsewhere – that is the round of existence.

Buddhist text

In the Buddhist scriptures the human body is often compared to a house and the spirit to the guest who moves on when the house has served its purpose. Buddha taught that the soul is not a single entity but a composite of five elements – the physical body, the emotions, the senses, willpower and consciousness, which dissolve at the moment of death, leaving only pure consciousness (*rupa*).

The immediate source of a mind... must be a mind which existed before the conception took place; the mind must have a continuity from a previous mind. This we hold to prove the existence of a past life.

The Dalai Lama

Each of our lives is connected by a common theme (a lesson we must learn) ensuring a certain continuity, but it is our essence not our personality which is transmitted from body to body in much the same way that one candle can be used to light another before it is extinguished. When the divine flame is re-ignited in a new body it brings a new personality into being, but in Buddhism this personality with which we identify, and which is the equivalent of the Ego, is simply a state of mind.

That said, Buddhists do speak of their former lives, which Western practitioners often find confusing and even contradictory. After all, if the personality dissolves upon the death of the body, why do Tibetan Buddhists seek out the reincarnation of their Dalai Lama, who will frequently demonstrate knowledge of his former life even while still a young boy? This

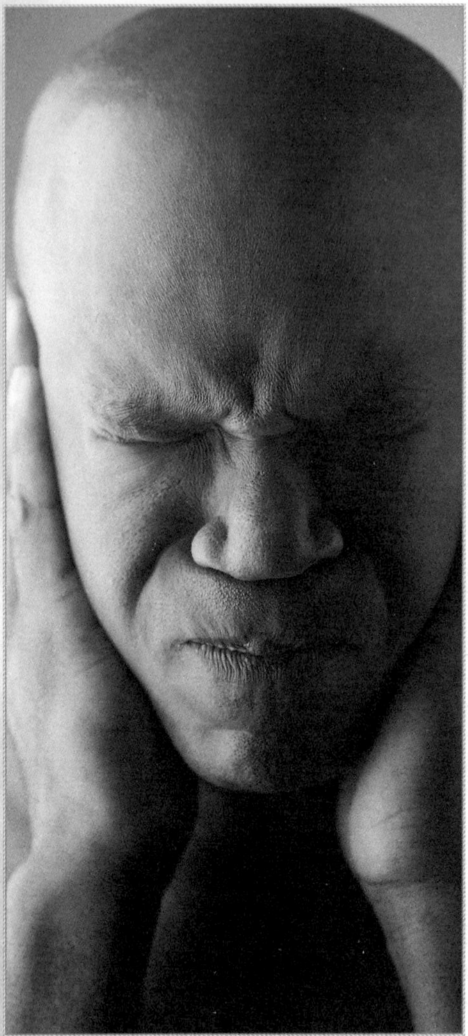

paradox evidently puzzled pupils of the Buddha, one of whom asked his master to clarify the situation.

> *Thou believest, O Master, that beings are reborn; that they migrate in the evolution of life; and that subject to the law of karma we must reap what we sow. Yet thou teachest the non-existence of the soul! Thy disciples praise utter self-extinction as the highest bliss of Nirvana. If I am merely a combination of the sankharas, my existence will cease when I die. If I am merely a compound of sensations and ideas and desires, whither can I go at the dissolution of the body?*

Said the Blessed One

> *O Brahman, thou art religious and earnest. Thou art seriously concerned about thy soul. Yet is thy work in vain because thou art lacking in the one thing that is needful.*
>
> *There is rebirth of character, but no transmigration of a self. Thy thought-forms reappear, but there is no ego entity transferred. The stanza uttered by a teacher is reborn in the scholar who repeats the word.*

As for the law of karma, the universal law of cause and effect which determines the quality of each life, Buddha summed up it up by saying

Surely if living creatures saw the results of all their evil deeds, they would turn away from them in disgust…

> *For owners of their deeds (karma) are the beings, heirs of their deeds; their deeds are the womb from which they sprang; with their deeds they are bound up; their deeds are their refuge. Whatever deeds they do – good or evil – of such they will be the heirs. And wherever the beings spring into existence, there their deeds will ripen; and wherever their deeds ripen, there they will earn the fruits of those deeds, be it in this*

life, or be it in the next life, or be it in any other future life... Surely if living creatures saw the results of all their evil deeds, they would turn away from them in disgust. But selfhood blinds them, and they cling to their obnoxious desires. They crave pleasure for themselves and they cause pain to others; when death destroys their individuality, they find no peace; their thirst for existence abides and their selfhood reappears in new births. Thus they continue to move in the coil and can find no escape from the hell of their own making.

In *Meditation: The Inward Art* (Philadelphia, Lippincott 1963), Bradford Smith of Columbia University observed the striking similarity between the traditional Tibetan custom of seeking the reborn Dalai Lama and the Christian story:

When the previous Dalai Lama died, wise men had gone forth to seek the new Holy One, had found a little boy who recognized things that had belonged to his predecessor and could pick them out unerringly from among similar objects... so here is a religion where an infant is born obscurely, recognized by wise men and worshipped; where a Holy Man prophesies that he will return from the dead. Does this make me suspect Christianity? Good – face the doubt. Virgin birth, infant god, the Holy One violently killed, yet resurrected – these are repeated themes in the history of world religions...

These repetitions do not palliate or cancel the strength of the Christian story. Rather they are reinforcing examples of the universal religious impulse and of the way man seeks to represent the cycle of death and rebirth that runs through all of nature. In Tibetan Buddhism, with its firm faith in the rebirth of the soul, not only of Dalai Lamas but of all, and of a progress based upon behaviour during past lives, this impulse is dramatically present.

Lingerh the Divine Child in 1940: he is said to have been born at the exact moment the 13th Dalai Lama died, but never succeeded him

The Tibetans put their belief in reincarnation into practice every time they seek out the successor to the deceased Dalai Lama. In fact, the process of identifying the reborn soul in the present Dalai Lama was described in *The Spectator*, October 1973.

> *In the 'Wood Hog' year of 1935 the [acting] regent saw in a vision three letters of the Tibetan alphabet; a monastery with a roof of jade green and gold; and a house with turquoise tiles. A detailed description of the vision was written down and kept secret. When Tibet's wise men… travelled eastwards in search of the new born babe they found him in the village of Taktser, in Ando Province in north East Tibet, in a turquoise tiled house next to a green and gold roofed monastery.*
>
> *But the real test for reincarnation is whether he can recall men and matters from a previous life, thereby demonstrating the triumphant transmigration of the soul. So the leader of Tibet's wise men disguised himself as a servant, and his servant as the leader, and entered the 'house of the turquoise roof'. The unsuspecting parents invited the 'leader' of the party into their respected altar room while the 'servant' went to the kitchen – where a two-year-old child was playing. The disguised leader was wearing a rosary round his neck that had belonged to the 13th Dalai Lama, and the child asked to be given it. Surprised but alert the leader promised to give it to the boy child if he could guess who he was. The toddler replied that he was 'seraaga,' which, in the local dialect meant a Lama of Sera monastery in Lhasa. This was correct and to the mounting excitement of the search party he proceeded to name them all correctly. [Then followed other difficult tests, which the boy easily passed.]*

'Buddhists do not mourn the loss of a loved one, but celebrate the spirit's release from suffering'

The Tibetan Book of the Dead

The hour has come to part with this body, composed of flesh and blood;
May I know the body to be impermanent and illusory.

The Tibetan Book of the Dead

THE BUDDHISTS have a pragmatic attitude to death. They do not mourn the loss of a loved one, but celebrate the spirit's release from the suffering of this earthly life. This attitude is not dictated by religious doctrine, nor conditioned by a culture which lacks compassion or sentiment. On the contrary, the Buddhist culture values compassion as a divine attribute and a quality to be nurtured. The Buddhist disregard for grief is simply a consequence of their knowledge of the process of death

A funeral procession in north-east India, 1982, as monks carry the body of Rigpe Dorje, the 16th karmapa, *to Rumtek Monastery*

and rebirth. For the Buddhist the process is no more a mystery than the life cycle of the butterfly is to the naturalist and this understanding comes mainly from a remarkable document which offers explicit instructions for easing their passing from this world to the next.

The Tibetan Book of the Dead (a funerary text attributed to Padmasambhava, the founder of Tantric Buddhism), was intended to be read aloud by those who watched over the dead on 49 successive days – this being the period during which the soul is believed to linger in the Bardo, the intermediate state between death and rebirth. Though it was written more than a thousand years ago, its description of the three stages of death are uncannily similar to modern accounts of NDEs.

The first stage, called *'chikai bardo'*, occurs when consciousness is suspended at the point of separation from the physical body. At this moment individuals are unaware that they are dead. Only when they look down on their own lifeless bodies do they realize that this ethereal essence is their true self.

> *Thine intellect hath been separated from thy body. Because of this inability to loiter, thou oft-times wilt feel perturbed and vexed and panic-stricken...*

The Tibetan Book of the Dead *is not a single text. Rather it is a collection of writings on consciousness after death but before rebirth*

There follows a detailed description of the etheric body and its capabilities:

Having a body [seemingly] fleshly [resembling] the former and that to
be produced,
Endowed with all sense faculties and power of unimpeded motion.

During the dissolution discarnate personalities may be subjected to hallucinations that invite comparison with the tunnel of light described by those who claim to have had a NDE.

The reading of the relevant passages is intended to familiarize them with their new reality for as in NDEs they can still hear and see the living although they themselves cannot be seen or heard.

The next stage is crucial if the spirit is to be free to enter the 'clear, primordial light' of the higher world. The following passages stress the importance of the letting go of all emotional attachments to people and places so that the soul may ascend into the light.

But some may be unwilling, or unable, to relinquish their possessions or may harbour regrets or resentment which will effectively bind them to the earthly plane. Others may be literally haunted by their own evil deeds. They will only exorcize these memories by reliving them in a succession of hells of their own making.

O now, when the Bardo of Reality upon me is dawning!
Abandoning all awe, fear, and terror of all phenomena,
May I recognize whatever appears as being my own thought-forms,
May I know them to be apparitions in the intermediate state.

Having faced the consequences of their actions they can then submit to the mercy of the Buddha within, their own divine essence who determines whether they can enter Nirvana or must reincarnate. Assuming that most souls will need to return to the world for further trials the concluding prayers are intended to guide them to re-enter under the most favourable circumstances.

O procrastinating one, who thinks not
of the coming of death,
Devoting yourself to the useless
doings of this life,
Improvident are you in dissipating
your great opportunity;

Mistaken, indeed, will your purpose
be now if you return empty-handed
from this life.

The Tibetan Book of The Dead
(Evans-Wentz translation)

The most significant difference between the Buddhist concept of rebirth and that of other traditions is that Buddhists believe that there are many states of being (many heavens and many hells) and that a soul gravitates to the level to which it is attracted. A psychologically disturbed individual, for example, will remain a restless spirit when freed from the body and will descend to the realm of the hungry ghosts, which like-minded souls inhabit, and will wallow in a hell of its own making. For this reason, suicide is considered to solve nothing – it will only delay the soul's development.

The difference between Buddhism and other traditions is that Buddhists believe in many states of being (many heavens and many hells)

Those who are addicted to alcohol, drugs and possessions will indulge themselves until they realize their craving will never be satisfied

Those who are addicted to alcohol, drugs and possessions will likewise be bound to this dream-like state where they can indulge themselves until they finally awaken to the realization that their craving will never be satisfied and that what they are really suffering from is their separation from the source – the divine.

When this state of awareness is attained the soul has the opportunity to relinquish its cravings and break free. It can then return to Earth to complete its series of lives. Conversely, those who attain enlightenment during their lifetimes – that is, mastery of their bodies, thoughts and emotions – will immediately ascend to the higher realms from where they can influence the course of human evolution as *Bodhisattvas* (enlightened souls).

✣ ISLAM ✣

Like grass I have grown over and over again. I passed out of mineral form and lived as a plant. From plant I was lifted up to be an animal. Then I put away the animal form and took on a human shape. Why should I fear that if I died I shall be lost?

Jalal al-Din Rumi

ISLAM REJECTS the idea of reincarnation, although there are several clear references to it in the Koran, the sacred text channelled by the prophet Mohammed from AD 610 onwards. Sufi mystics, such as the thirteenth century poet Jalal al-Din Rumi (1207–73), considered themselves custodians of the true teachings of their prophet, which they understood to advocate universal brotherhood, but their stance only incurred the wrath of the self-righteous who condemned them as heretics. In their own defence, the Sufis would cite several passages of the Koran in support of their interpretation of the teachings. This also served as a warning to their fellow Muslims of the dangers of religious intolerance. Perhaps the most convincing of these was:

Rumi was a Persian scholar who lived most of his life in Anatolia. After he died, his followers founded the Mevlevi Order or 'Whirling Dervishes'

> *People of the book do not go to excess in your religion, do not say of God anything but truth. The Messiah, Jesus son of Mary was only an envoy of God and a word of God bestowed upon Mary and a spirit of God.*
>
> *Koran 5:69*

Other verses explicitly speak of the existence of the soul but traditionalists would argue that these could be read as referring to the physical resurrection at the End of Days.

> *And Allah hath caused you to spring forth from the Earth*
> *like a plant;*

Hereafter will He turn you back into it again, and bring you forth anew.

Koran 71:17–18

And again:

Thou [God] makest the night to pass into the day and Thou makest the day to pass into the night, and Thou bringest forth the living from the dead and Thou bringest forth the dead from the living, and Thou givest sustenance to whom Thou pleasest without measure.

Koran 3:28

Elsewhere the allusion to reincarnation seems explicit:

And when his body falleth off altogether, as an old fish shell, his soul doeth well by releasing, and formeth a new one instead… the person of man is only a mask which the soul putteth on for a season; it weareth its proper time and then is cast off and another is worn in its stead.

New Koran

God generates beings, and sends them back over and over again, till they return to him.

Koran 2:28

The Sufis would say that even devout Muslims must harbour doubts as to how that prediction could be fulfilled, if one acknowledges the effects of corruption and the fact that those who die a violent death are rarely interred intact. However, the many references to the existence of the soul defy one to deny it:

How can you make denial of Allah, who made you live again when you died, will make you dead again, and then alive again, until you finally return to him?

Koran 2:28

God is the one who created you all, then provided you sustenance, then will cause you to die, then will bring you to life.

Koran 11:38

'God is the one who created you all, then provided you sustenance, then will cause you to die, then will bring you to life'

‘Like the sun, only when you set in the West can you rise again with brilliance in the East’

Surely it is God who splits the seed and the stone, bringing the living from the dead; and it is God who brings the dead from the living.

Koran 6:95

I tell you, of a truth, that the spirits which now have affinity shall be kindred together, although they all meet in new persons and names.

New Koran

It seems that if Orthodox Islam could be said to share anything with Judaism and Christianity it is a distrust of those who ask it to re-examine its esoteric origins and their desire to preserve its traditions at any price.

The Sufi mystics, ever conscious of their sacred duty to reveal the inner truths of Islamic wisdom, as they saw it, persisted in promoting the idea in their poetry and prose, even if their lives were at risk.

There have been thousands of changes in form. Look always to the form in the present; for, if you think of the forms in the past, you will separate yourself from your true Self. These are all states of the permanent which you have seen by dying. Why then do you turn your face from death? Die happily and look forward to taking up a new and better form. Like the sun, only when you set in the West can you rise again with brilliance in the East.

Jalal al-Din Rumi, Mathnawi

✣ Judaism ✣

If a man dies, shall he live again?

Job (14:14)

Though modern orthodox Jews reject the possibility of reincarnation, it is likely that it was once part of secret teachings within Judaic traditions

MODERN ORTHODOX Judaism rejects the possibility of reincarnation, although traditional Jewish services feature prayers asking for forgiveness for sins committed in both the present life and in previous incarnations. Despite the refusal of leading rabbinical authorities to accept reincarnation, the Jewish esoteric tradition embraces the idea.

The Jewish mystics were never content with blind faith and empty ritual. They desired personal experience of the upper worlds and did so by attaining altered states of awareness through a meditation technique they called *Merkabah* ('rising in the chariot'), which forms the basis of visualizations practised by modern day Kabbalists. These once secret teachings are believed to have been practised in biblical times by ascetic sects such as the Nazarenes and the Essenes, of whom Joshua ben Miriam (Jesus) and Saul of Tarsus (St Paul) are believed to have been initiates.

Rabbi Manasseh ben Israel (1604–57) wrote:

> *The belief or the doctrine of the transmigration of souls is a firm and infallible dogma accepted by the whole assemblage of our faith with one accord, so that there is none to be found who would dare to deny it... indeed, there are a great number of sages in Israel who hold firm to this doctrine so that they make it a dogma, a fundamental point of our religion. We are therefore in duty bound to obey and to accept this dogma with acclamation... as the truth of it has been incontestably demonstrated by the Zohar, and all books of the Kabbalists.*

The Old Testament contains several significant verses which appear to refer to reincarnation, specifically the notion that the prophets were reborn in new bodies to continue their work.

> *And when the sons of the prophets which were to view at Jericho saw him, they said 'The spirit of Elijah doth rest on Elisha'. And they came to meet him and bowed themselves to the ground before him.*
>
> *2 Kings (2:15)*

Even in the more obscure passages the implication is clear, that human life regenerates as readily as the grass.

> *Thou carriest them away as with a flood; they are as a sleep: in the morning they are like grass which groweth up.*
>
> *Psalms (90:2–5)*

There is also the promise of release from the cycle of death and rebirth for those who learn the lessons of life.

> *Him that overcometh will I make a pillar in the temple of my God, and he shall go no more out.*
>
> *Revelations (3:12)*

The Jewish historian and soldier Flavius Josephus (AD 37–100) was recorded as having urged his men to fight by promising them an easy life next time if they should die in battle:

> *Do ye not remember that all pure spirits when they depart out of this life obtain a most holy place in heaven, from whence, in the*

revolutions of ages, they are again sent into pure bodies.

According to the Zohar, which is thought to have been compiled in AD80 but to have been augmented by a succession of scholars through the centuries, before being published by Rabbi Moses de Leon in 1280:

All souls are subject to the trials of transmigration and men do not know the designs of the Most High with regard to them; they know not how they are being at all times judged, both before coming into this world and when they leave it. They do not know how many transmigrations and mysterious trials they must undergo. Souls must re-enter the absolute substance whence they have emerged. But to accomplish this end they must develop all the perfections, the germ of which is planted in them; and if they have not fulfilled this condition during one life, they must commence another, a third, and so forth, until they have acquired the condition which fits them for reunion with God.

Jewish historian and soldier Flavius Josephus who urged his men into battle with promises of an easy life next time if they should die in action

Reincarnation of a Rich Man

THE JEWISH PEOPLE'S ambivalent attitude toward reincarnation is revealed in this traditional Hasidic story which appears in the *Karliner Hasidim*. When Rabbi Aharon of Karlin died young his pupil, Reb Shlomo, was appointed his successor. But instead of welcoming his new status Shlomo expressed his reluctance to take on the responsibility. On the one hand he doubted whether he was worthy of the task and on a personal level he dreaded being hounded by members of his community at all hours of the day and night as Rabbi Aharon had been.

'I don't want such fame and responsibility,' Shlomo protested. 'I just want to lead a private life as an ordinary Jew.'

So the Karliner Hasidim were left without a Rabbi. But the spirit of Rabbi Aharon would not rest and appeared to Shlomo in a dream.

'Shlomo, my friend and dearest student,' said the spirit, 'if you will take on the yoke of leadership, you will be granted the power of seeing all the wanderings of souls in their various incarnations.'

Reb Shlomo was thrilled at the prospect of inheriting such a talent and so willingly agreed to accept the role of Rabbi of Karlin. In the following days Shlomo delighted in his new gift, viewing the past lives of any person he chose simply by expressing his desire to do so. He also discovered that this insight gave him the means of identifying the nature of their present problems which were derived from their actions in former incarnations and even divining their future lives.

Using his gift for second sight Rabbi Shlomo saw that the soul of the rich man was destined to be reborn as the poor woman's son

But before the day had ended the Rabbi found himself with a seemingly unsolvable dilemma. Two messengers came to his house, each with a request for a miracle. The first had been sent by a dying merchant with a generous donation for the synagogue and a letter begging the Rabbi to pray for a miracle to save his life.

The second was from a poor woman who was suffering the pangs of labour and feared she would die as she could not deliver the child. Using his gift for second sight Rabbi Shlomo saw that the soul of the rich man was destined to be reborn as the poor woman's son.

With that knowledge, he prayed that the will of God be carried out without delay. By nightfall the rich man had expired and his soul had entered the body of the poor woman's baby which had miraculously been delivered without further complications.

But the matter was not over yet. The following day news reached the Rabbi that the mother and infant had no firewood and were in danger of freezing to death so the Rabbi used some of the merchant's donation to buy them provisions and gave the balance of the money to the mother for the child's care. After all, was it not the boy's own money?

Nothing more was heard of the pair until six years later when they returned to the town having spent what was left of the money. They were again reduced to begging for their meals and lodging. Coincidentally, their return coincided with a party for the rich man's eldest son who was celebrating his bar mitzvah (entry into adulthood). It was customary to invite the poor to these celebrations and so the boy and his mother attended the festivities.

But on entering the house the boy demanded to sit at the top table and made such a commotion that the Rabbi begged the hostess to humour him. But the boy's behaviour did not improve. He demanded the choicest cuts of the meat and he refused to accept the pennies that were handed out to the poor at the end of the party. He demanded the gold that he had hoarded in his earlier incarnation as the head of the house. At that the family had him thrown into the street. Rabbi Shlomo could not bear to see the family treat their 'father' in such a fashion and knowing that this would not be the last such incident he would be forced to witness, he prayed to God to take away his powers.

The Mystery Revealed?

PRACTITIONERS OF the Jewish mystical tradition known as Kabbalah believe that they have been entrusted with the mysteries of life and death. For centuries they took an oath to share the secret only with fellow initiates, but today Kabbalah has become fashionable among spiritual seekers of all faiths and its teachings are available to anyone who is interested enough to attend the numerous courses on offer. Its once jealously guarded magical system is now available over the counter at any bookstore.

Kabbalah is the ancient Jewish metaphysical philosophy that seeks to explain our place and purpose in existence through a symbolic diagram known as the Tree of Life, on which are arranged the divine attributes of the Creator (see diagram on page 49). These complementary qualities are also manifest in finite form in every human being, but we need to become conscious of these characteristics and bring them into balance to become fully realized and enlightened beings.

'According to Kabbalistic tradition, each human soul is a spark of the Divine'

According to Kabbalistic tradition, each human soul is a spark of the Divine, which acquired bodies of increasing density during its descent into matter. Each individual comprises four elements, therefore – a physical body, a psyche, a vital soul and the divine spark of pure consciousness. Kabbalists consider Out Of Body Experiences (OBEs) to be simply a temporary detachment between the physical body and the psyche, whereas death involves a permanent separation.

Death occurs when the vital soul (Nefesh) can no longer hold the physical body and its etheric double, the psyche, in synchronization. This

A Jewish funeral is conducted with simple dignity. The coffin is made of pine and the body is wrapped in a white shroud

may be because of a prolonged illness which weakens an individual's hold on life or a violent act which wrenches the two apart. At this stage the umbilical silver cord of etheric energy linking the psyche to the body separates, in a reversal of the birth process, at the point where the centre of consciousness corresponding to knowledge of the body (known as Daat, the unmanifest attribute on the Tree of Life) was joined to the lower self or ego centre on the psyche (known as Yesod or the Foundation) [see diagram opposite].

So strong is the empathic link between the two elements that it is not uncommon for the psyche to remain within the vicinity of the body for several days, which would explain the many sightings of the deceased at their own funeral. In the Jewish tradition this apparition is known as the *Zelim*, or shadow image, but it is common to all cultures, hence the universal custom of ritual farewells to ease its passing into the next world.

Those souls who are unable, or unwilling, to ascend to the next level, because of attachments, addictions or a determination to resolve unfinished business, remain earthbound and may be perceived as ghosts. Others may simply be unaware that they are dead, either because they could not conceive of a life after death, or because they were unprepared. Until they are made aware of the fact that they no longer have an impact on the physical world they may habitually relive their daily routines.

Those few souls who experience the symbolic state we call Purgatory are bringing this mode of existence into being in a form that conforms to their beliefs, so that they can indulge their need to castigate themselves for their actions on earth. It is significant and revealing that Purgatory is traditionally envisaged in terms of the four elements (boiling mud, ice, fire, lack of water, etc.) because this illusion is generated by the forces operating in the 'pit' of the Yeziratic or emotional world or, to put it in psychological terms, in the egocentric region of the psyche.

But according to the Kabbalah the majority of us will recuperate from life's trials at the centre of the Yeziratic world, in the Heavenly Eden, while more advanced souls will ascend to the realm of pure spirit (Beriah, the world of Creation). Only these highly developed souls can chose the time of their next incarnation for they are self-aware and know what tasks they need to accomplish and what experiences they need.

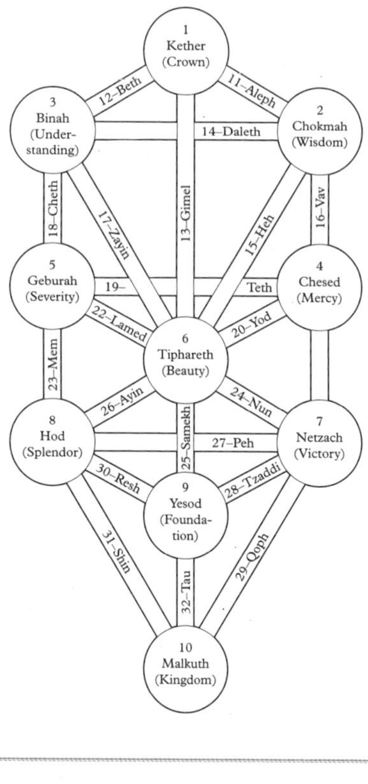

THE TREE OF LIFE

Kether: *Essence/Seed/ Potential – the Divine Plan*
Chokmah: *Divine Reality – the Cosmic Computer*
Binah: *Nurtures Potential, Gives Birth to the Temporal*
Chesed: *Intention to Emulate the Creator*
Geburah: *Determination to Realize the Vision*
Tiphareth: *Balance and Symmetry Prefacing Success*
Netzach: *Action and Effort, Contemplation*
Hod: *Vision which Elaborates with Observation*
Yesod: *All-engrossing Creative State, Coherent Knowledge*
Malkuth: *Realization of Divine Plan, Unlimited Bounty through Invention*

✣ CHRISTIANITY ✣

Our Lord has written the promise of the resurrection,
not in books alone but in every leaf in springtime...
In our sad condition our only consolation is
the expectancy of another life.

Martin Luther

Above: Martin Luther (1483–1546). Opposite: 'Angels Rolling Away the Stone from the Sepulchre' by William Blake (1777-1827)

CONTRARY TO POPULAR belief reincarnation was a core concept in the early years of Christianity, but it was cynically and wilfully airbrushed out of the teachings by the Roman emperor Justinian in AD 533.

The New Testament notes that at the time of Jesus the Jews were awaiting the arrival of their Messiah whose appearance would be announced by the prophet Elias (Elijah) who would return to earth in a new form. Before he declared himself to be the Son of God, Jesus was frequently identified by his followers as the reincarnation of a prophet. In the Gospel of Matthew he is told:

Some say thou art John the Baptist, some Elias; and others Jeremias or one of the prophets.

Matthew 16:13–4

Herod is also quoted as suspecting that Jesus might be the evangelist whom he had recently beheaded.

Jesus is said to have confirmed that the coming of the Messiah would be preceded by the reappearance of Elias but added:

Elias is come already, and they know him not... Then the disciples understood that he spake to them of John the Baptist.

Matthew 17:12–13

A reference to the identity of Elias also appears in an earlier chapter.

Among them that are born of women there hath not risen a greater than John the Baptist... And if ye will receive it this is Elias...

Matthew 11:11,14

During his ministry Jesus himself made several allusions to reincarnation and the law of karma, most notably when he declared, 'As you sow, so shall you reap'. He also proclaimed that the kingdom of heaven is within every man and not in the heavens, by which it is understood that he was referring to the divine spirit.

Resurrection

THE PROMISE OF a physical resurrection is an invention of the Church contrary to the teachings of Jesus and the disciples who spoke of ascending to heaven in spirit after having discarded the physical body upon death. According to the Gnostic gospels, Jesus appeared to his followers in spirit to prove that the soul survives death, but because of the selective editing of the gospels by those with a vested interest in keeping the Church's monopoly on salvation this central teaching was taken literally.

In 1 Corinthians (15:50) and Peter (1:1:18) it is stated that flesh and blood cannot enter the celestial kingdom, while in John 3:13 it is noted that heaven is for spiritual beings and that we are all spirit in essence and will return from whence we came.

And no man hath ascended up to heaven, but he that came down from the heaven, even the Son of man which is in heaven.

St Paul attempted to clarify the idea that Jesus had risen physically from the tomb and in so doing made a distinction between our earthly form and our spirit.

There are also celestial bodies, and bodies terrestrial: but the glory of the celestial is one, and the glory of the terrestrial is another... There is a natural body and there is a spiritual body.

1 Corinthians 15:35–44

In 2 Corinthians St Paul describes his ascent 'in the spirit' to the third heaven by which Orthodox Christians understand him to be referring to the Empyriam, the kingdom of God (the first heaven being the physical firmament of sky and stars; the second heaven being where the souls of the righteous dwell). But St Paul was an initiate of the Merkabah (a form of Jewish mysticism) and did not intend for his reference to three heavens to be taken literally. In the Merkabah the three heavens are the three upper worlds of Emanation, Creation and Formation, corresponding to the emotional, mental and spiritual dimensions which can be explored through the spiritual discipline of meditation which can facilitate the separation of spirit and body.

Soul Travel

AFTER THE CRUCIFIXION the belief in the human soul and its ability to enter a new body remained a central tenet of the teachings of the early Church. St Jerome, who was regarded as the greatest authority on Christian doctrine after the Apostles, made explicit reference to the soul's existence prior to birth, as did St Justin Martyr (AD100–165) who spoke explicitly of reincarnation. Origen (*c.* AD185–254), a founding father of Christian theology, promoted the belief that religious intolerance was self-defeating, both for the Church and for its followers, because every human being would be born into the culture and religion of his neighbour, and even his enemies, over the course of many lifetimes.

> *Everyone, therefore, of those who descend to the earth is, according to his deserts or to the position that he had there, ordained to be born in this world either in a different place, or in a different nation, or in a different occupation, or with different infirmities, or to be descended from religious or at least less pious parents; so as sometimes to bring about that an Israelite descends among the Scythians, and a poor Egyptian is brought down to Judaea.*
>
> *De Principiis IV, Cap. 3, 10, 26, 23*

'Every soul comes into this world strengthened by the victories or weakened by the defeats of its previous life'

St Gregory, Bishop of Nyssa (AD 331–395) was equally explicit in his endorsement of the belief.

> *Every soul comes into this world strengthened by the victories or weakened by the defeats of its previous life… The soul… is immaterial and invisible in nature, it at one time puts off one body… and exchanges it for a second.*

St Augustine (AD 354–430) apparently delighted in regaling his followers with the allegedly true story of Senator Curma whose spirit left his body as he lay in a coma. On hearing his name being called he went in search of other spirits, thinking he had been summoned for the Last Judgment. They told him that it was another man with the same name who was being called to heaven, a goldsmith who lived in the same town. After wandering aimlessly in this netherworld he met the spirits of people he knew to be still alive, so they were presumably dreaming at that moment. When he finally

returned to his body he sent a servant to the house of Curma the goldsmith and was told that the man had died that very day.

But not everyone in the Church was amused by such stories.

Father Synesius, Bishop of Ptolemais (*c.*AD 370–430) was one of many of the Church's founding fathers to speak openly of reincarnation and in doing so created the schism which one hundred years later led to the removal of the concept from official Christian doctrine. He wrote:

Philosophy speaks of souls being prepared by a course of transmigrations… When first it comes down to Earth, it (the soul) embarks on this animal spirit as on a boat and through it is brought into contact with matter.

Above: the Devil hands St Augustine The Book of Vices. Below: Constantine the Great, who split the Christian Church into warring factions

A Theological Coup

THE UNSEEMLY SQUABBLE between the pro-reincarnation lobby and its detractors was more of a political row than a theological argument. It originated in AD 330 when Constantine the Great relocated the capital of the Roman Empire from Rome to Constantinople in an attempt to exert his authority over the Christian population under his control. Thereafter the Church split into two warring factions with Constantine determining the doctrine of the Eastern branch of the Church and the authorities in Rome issuing their own decrees as to what constituted true Christianity.

By the sixth century the split had become acrimonious in the extreme with Emperor Justinian, the new ruler of Constantinople, going so far as to excommunicate those who openly defied him. And one topic which proved particularly divisive was reincarnation. To silence the dissenting voices Justinian staged what amounted to a theological coup by convening an Ecumenical Council in AD533 and inviting 159 bishops from the Eastern Church, whom he knew he could count on to endorse his decision, but only six from the Western Church. The Pope protested, but was powerless to prevent Justinian from forcing through his amendments and so, at a stroke, a core teaching of Jesus and his disciples was written out of Christian doctrine.

After this not even the most learned theological scholars dared to contravene the edict for fear of being declared a heretic, which would almost certainly have meant excommunication, torture and death. But even the emperor's displeasure could not reverse the laws of nature nor suppress the legends surrounding the saints – among them St Severns of Ravenna, St Ambrose and St Clement of Rome – who, it was said, were able to preach in one church while their spirits were seen at another location. St Anthony of Padua was said to have been preaching in Limoges, France, in 1226 when he remembered that he had agreed to attend a nearby monastery. In full view of the congregation, he knelt in silent prayer for several minutes. At the same time he appeared before the monks in another district of the town, where they heard him read the lesson as he had promised, before vanishing before their eyes. Over 500 years later, in 1774, St Alphonsus Liguori remained unconscious for 24 hours after collapsing during Mass. On recovering he claimed to have been present at the death of Pope Clement XIV in Rome, where he had been seen at the bedside by the assembled dignitaries, praying for the pontiff.

St Anthony of Padua was a preacher of great skill and eloquence. It is said that few could sit through his sermons unmoved

How can a world progress in inner things... if the birth of each new generation fills the world with unregenerate souls full of original sin?

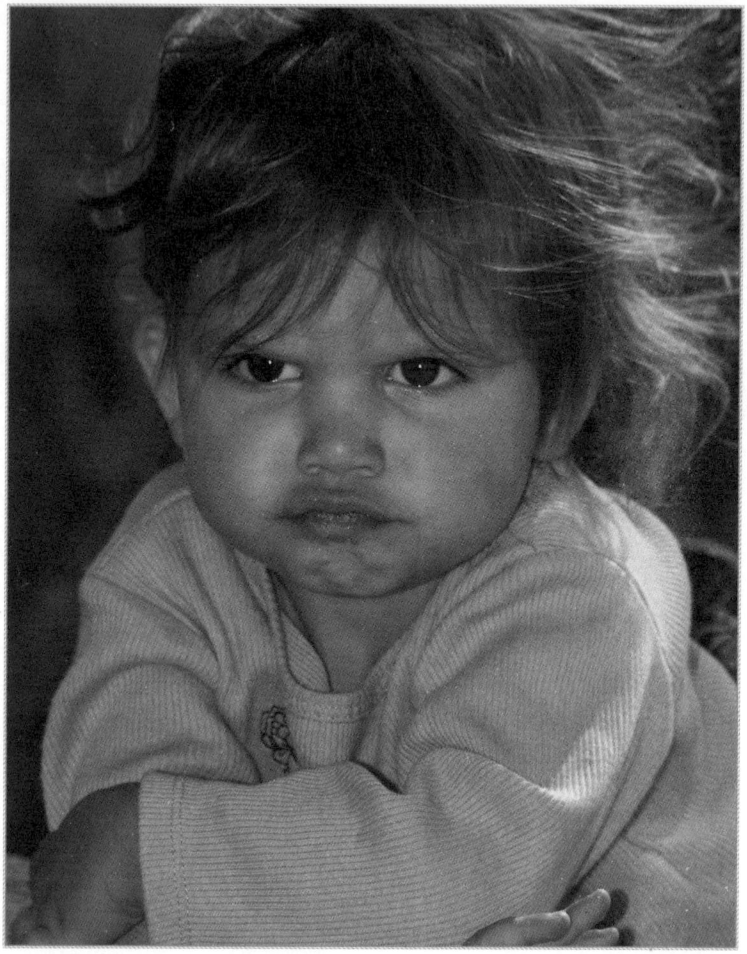

Such stories may strike the non-believer as prime examples of Catholic mythology, but the phenomenon, known as bilocation, is acknowledged by science. Meanwhile, despite Church edicts to the contrary, conscientious Christians continue to interpret the scriptures according to their own beliefs.

The Reverend Leslie Weatherhead, an ardent advocate of free thinking in theological matters, stated the case in his influential lecture, 'The Case For Reincarnation'.

The intelligent Christian asks not only that life should be just, but that it should make sense. Does the idea of reincarnation help here? If I failed to pass those examinations in life which can only be taken while I dwell in a physical body, shall I not have to come back and take them again? If every birth in the world is the birth of a new soul, I don't see how progress can ever be consummated. Each has to begin at scratch. Each child is born a selfish little animal, not able in character to begin where the most saintly parent left off. How can a world progress in inner things – which are the most important – if the birth of every new generation fills the world with unregenerate souls full of original sin? There can never be a perfect world unless those gradually born into it can take advantage of lessons learned in earlier lives instead of starting at scratch.

II

Into the Light

I am confident that there truly is such a thing as living again, that the living spring from the dead, and that the souls of the dead are in existence.

Socrates

IF THERE IS one question that could truly be said to concern us all, it is the enduring mystery of life after death. Namely, what happens when we die and what – if anything – awaits us in the world beyond? Crossing the 'final frontier' is the one fate we all share, the one fear or anxiety that haunts us throughout our lives. However, despite our increasing understanding of the nature of consciousness and the working of the human brain, it is a question for which orthodox science can provide no proof, on which philosophy can only speculate and to which religion is forced to demand blind faith.

And yet, there are those who claim to know the answer. Better still, they say that they have had a personal experience of the process of dying and have returned to tell the tale.

✤ LIVING GHOSTS ✤

It appears to me impossible that I should cease to exist, or that this active, restless spirit, equally alive to joy and sorrow, should be only organized dust – ready to fly abroad the moment the spring snaps, or the spark goes out, which kept it together. Surely something resides in this heart that is not perishable – and life is more than a dream.

Mary Wollstonecraft

Above: Mary Wollstonecraft (1759–1797) was a writer, philosopher and proto-feminist. Her daughter was Mary Shelley

IF REINCARNATION is a reality then there has to be some more tangible form of proof than the anecdotal evidence of those who claim to have recalled impressions from their former lives during regression. Fortunately we have a wealth of the personal accounts of those who claim to have had out-of-body experiences. Their claims are all the more credible because they are individuals with diverse backgrounds and beliefs, some of whom did not actually believe in life after death before their extraordinary experience. Moreover, some of these individuals were able to corroborate their claims by describing the scene at the time and the efforts of those who successfully resuscitated them when they were clinically dead.

The earliest surviving account of a Near Death Experience is that of an unnamed Northumbrian man, whose story was recorded by Saint Bede (*c.*673–735) in his *History of the English Church and People.*

A handsome man in a shining robe was my guide... He said to me... 'You must now return to your body and live among men once more; but, if you will weigh your actions with greater care and study to keep your words and ways virtuous and simple, then when you die you too will win a home among these happy spirits that you see'... I was most reluctant to return to my body ... but I did not dare to question my guide. Meanwhile, I know not how, I suddenly found myself alive among men once more.

The Venerable Bede (c. 673–735) was a widely travelled theologian and scholar who produced one of the earliest histories of England

St Bede adds that the man was so inspired by this promise of paradise that he devoted the rest of his life to spreading the good news.

> *Inspired by an insatiable longing for the blessings of heaven, and by his words and by his life, he helped many people to salvation.*

There must have been innumerable cases of a similar nature in earlier centuries that were not recorded, simply because few individuals outside the Church were capable of reading and writing. For this reason the phenomenon did not really come to light until the spiritualist movement brought it to public notice in the mid nineteenth century along with table-turning, apports (the materialization of objects out of thin air) and other paranormal phenomena.

The Reverend Bertrand realized he had lost all feeling in his hands. His first instinct was to accept the inevitable and pray

The unofficial voice of the movement was the Society for Psychical Research, formed in 1873 by a group of eminently respected members of the English academic world, including clergyman's son Frederick Myers and his mentor Professor Henry Sedgwick of Trinity College, Cambridge. They were later joined by two future prime ministers, the intellectual John Ruskin and several literary giants including the poet Alfred Lord Tennyson, American writer Mark Twain and Charles Lutwidge Dodgson, more commonly known as Lewis Carroll. The more romantic members might have been hoping for proof of the existence of spooks and fairies, but Myers and his more scientifically minded colleagues were determined to solve the mystery of life and death.

One of their more creditable investigations is relevant to the case in

favour of reincarnation because it was reported by a reputable source – a clergyman who described the actual physical process of dying, not only in detail but also objectively. It was originally published in the *Journal of Psychical Research* in 1892 and was supported by statements taken from those who were present and who were therefore able to verify the facts.

Frozen to Death

THE REVEREND BERTRAND was a seasoned alpine climber and therefore had no qualms about letting the other members of his party continue alone to the peak while he waited just below the summit for them to return. It was a crisp, clear day, ideal for mountaineering. But as he struck a match to light his cigar he realized that he had lost all feeling in his hands. In fact, he was unable to move at all. He realized that he was actually freezing to death. His first instinct was to accept the inevitable and pray, but having done so he decided there was nothing more he could do than observe the process of his own death.

Moments later he felt his conscious awareness separating from his physical shell, freeing him from pain and leaving him with the realization that his non-physical self was his real or true self while the body he had left behind had been discarded as easily as a worn-out coat. Then he noticed that he was still attached to this empty shell by what appeared to be an elastic string, which allowed him to float like a balloon.

Up he rose into the cloudless sky until he could look down on his fellow climbers who were taking the right hand path to the summit against his explicit instructions. He also saw the guide stop to take a chicken leg and a flask from the provisions he had lent him.

'Go on, old fellow,' he said to himself, 'eat the whole chicken if you choose, for I hope my miserable corpse will never eat or drink again.'

Drifting higher he could see the nearby town of Lungren, where he observed his wife enter a hotel with four fellow travellers. His only emotion at this point was regret that he could not sever the cord which bound him to his body and leave the earthly world behind. But before he could see what lay beyond this plane he was snapped back into his body, which was being vigorously massaged by the guide, who had returned from the summit and was making frantic efforts to restore his circulation.

'I had a hope – the balloon seemed much too big for the mouth. Suddenly I uttered an awful roar like a wild beast; the corpse swallowed the balloon, and Bertrand was Bertrand again.'

No one was inclined to believe his fantastic tale until he mentioned what he had seen – the guide taking the more dangerous track and sneaking a meal from his backpack and his wife making an unscheduled stop at the hotel, all of which were confirmed by those concerned.

'The lifeless figure in the bed was not the real Private Ritchie even though it looked like him and wore his fraternity ring'

The Phantom Soldier

ANOTHER 'TYPICAL' CASE, and one which is regarded as being highly significant in the study of paranormal phenomena, is that of Dr George Ritchie, a highly reputable psychiatrist whose experience was to inspire Dr Raymond Moody to initiate his seminal research on NDEs in the 1970s.

In December 1943 20-year-old Ritchie was serving as a private in the US Army and looking forward to a posting to the Army Medical School at Richmond, Virginia when he developed a high fever. The regimental doctor failed to diagnose his condition correctly and released him after prescribing aspirin to bring his temperature down. But Ritchie was suffering from double pneumonia and collapsed shortly after being admitted to hospital.

A senior doctor pronounced him dead and signed the death certificate, witnessed by a nurse, but Ritchie was very much alive. In fact, for the nine minutes that he was considered clinically dead he felt better than ever and all sense of sickness had left him. But he was confused to say the least. There he was, standing by his bed, trying in vain to tell the doctor that he was not dead, that the lifeless figure in the bed was not the real Private Ritchie even though it looked like him and wore his college fraternity ring.

'The slack jaw, the grey skin were awful,' he later recalled, but the thinking, vital essence of his being, his true self, was outside his body and still desperate to catch the train to his new posting in Richmond.

Confused, he left the room, moving through the ward in a dreamless state. In the hall he passed right through an orderly who seemed unaware of his presence.

'In some unimaginable way I had lost my firmness of flesh… the body that other people saw.'

He travelled some distance from the hospital before he accepted the fact that there was no point in getting to the medical school in Virginia if no one could see him. It was the certainty of knowing when you are dreaming and accepting the illogical aspect of the dreamworld, but Ritchie was acutely aware that he was not dreaming. The landscape he was passing through was real and he was fully conscious – more alert than ever in fact – but he was in a non-corporeal state which prevented him from interacting with the living. He must return to the hospital, he thought, and the thought itself was enough to take him there. The next instant he was searching from bed to bed looking for his physical counterpart. Although he no longer identified with the face that had once been so familiar, he knew he had to be reunited with his body, if only to enable him to move about the physical plane. At that moment he was between worlds. He thought he recognized a sleeping figure as his former self, but the ring was missing so he continued his frantic search until he came to a bed where a body lay draped in a sheet. This was the body he had vacated.

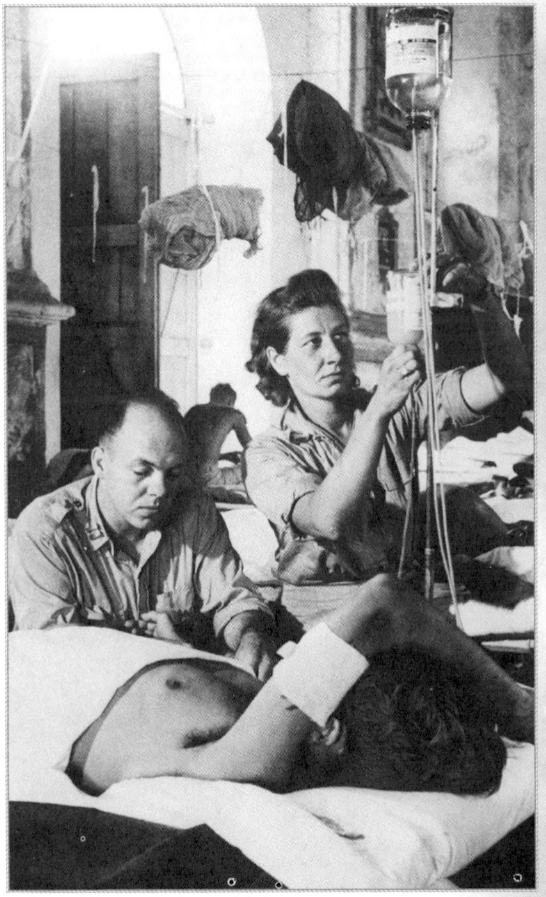

The regimental doctor failed to diagnose Ritchie's condition correctly and released him after prescribing aspirin to lower his temperature

'This is death,' he thought. 'This is what we human beings call "death", this splitting up of one's self.'

With that realization the room was bathed in white light and he sensed the overpowering presence of what he could only assume to be God. At that same instant his whole life passed before him, 'every event and thought and conversation, as palpable as a series of pictures'.

Now he was in another world, a greater reality than the one he had known. It was not heaven, nor was it hell. It was a netherworld, the Bardo of which the Buddhists speak, where lost souls continue with their routine lives, unaware that they are no longer living.

'To care most when you are most powerless: that would be hell indeed.'

He transcended this dimension by virtue of the fact that he was aware of his situation; and so he gravitated to higher states, but these too were not paradise or purgatory.

'They were too real, too solid.'

These worlds were not visions, but part of a greater reality, one he realized that he had not been aware of simply because he had been so preoccupied with the material world and his physical needs. Neither were they influenced by anything he had previously read on the subject because he had no interest in such matters at that time. With that realization he awoke in his body to the astonishment of the doctor and the nurse, who were preparing the corpse for the morgue.

According to conventional medical wisdom an individual who has been clinically dead for so long would have suffered irreparable brain damage, but Private George Ritchie had never felt better in his life.

Wernher von Braun has been called the 'father of the US space program', but being a scientist did not prevent his belief in an afterlife

Seeing Spirits

Everything science has taught me strengthens my belief in the continuity of our spiritual existence after death. I believe in an immortal soul. Science has proved that nothing disintegrates into nothingness. Life and soul, therefore, cannot disintegrate into nothingness, and so are immortal.

Wernher von Braun

DESPITE THE overwhelming number of Out Of Body Experiences (OBEs) and the fact that they all share the same core elements, orthodox scientists remain sceptical because there is no subjective test that can validate the existence of the astral or etheric body. Nevertheless, there have been several instances where a trained physician has observed what appears to be the soul's departure from the body during surgery. The experience of Chicago physician Dr Hout is just one such example.

Dr Hout told *Prediction* magazine that he had been 'privileged to see the spirit counterparts' of three patients. The first was of an elderly woman who had been brought into the theatre semi-conscious, the anaesthetic not yet having taken full effect.

> *As the anaesthetic deepened and the physical body became more relaxed, the freedom of the spirit body became greater. For the spirit form floated more freely away from the physical counterpart during the height of the anaesthetic. The spirit was quiet as if it was also in deep peaceful sleep.*

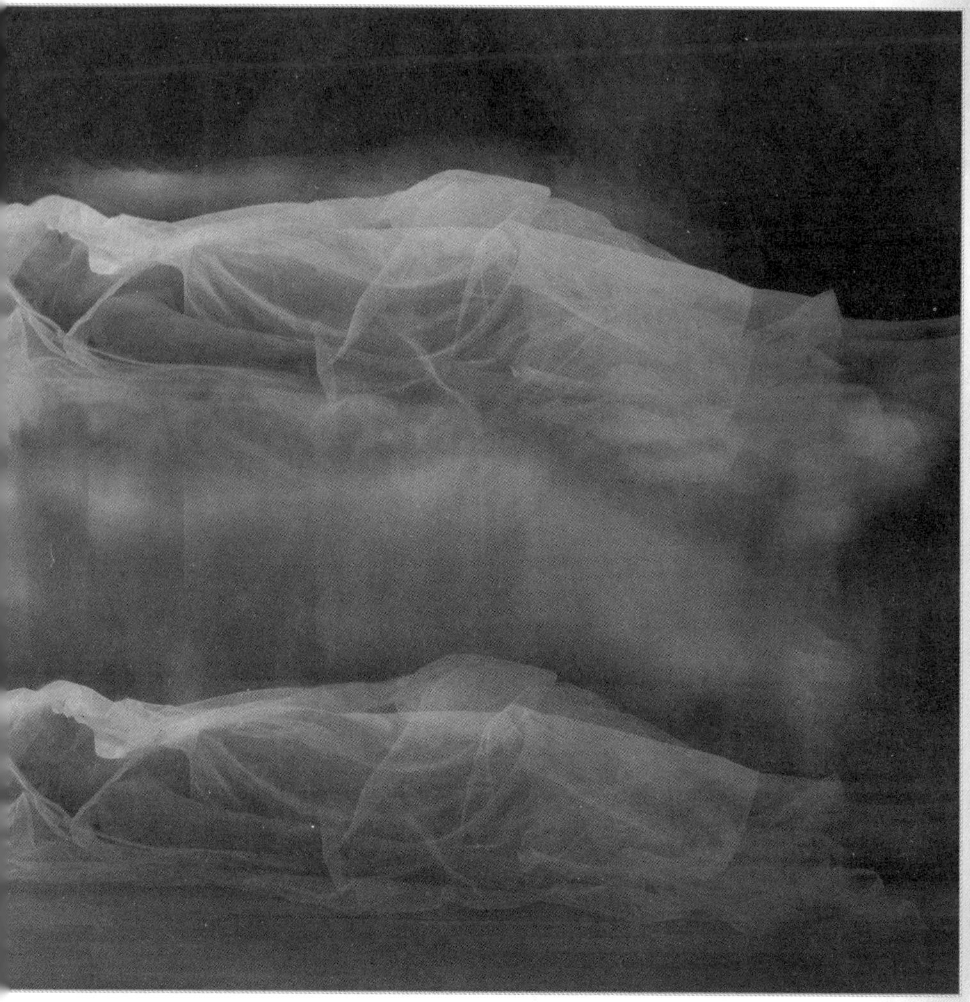

An elderly woman was brought into the theatre semi-conscious before the anaesthetic had taken full effect. It was then that her OBE began

Dr Hout was also able to see the silvery cord connecting the physical and etheric bodies which he described as a 'silvery shaft of light which wound around through the room in much the same way as a curl of smoke will drift indifferently in a still atmosphere'.

A British nurse, Joy Snell, had observed the same feature during the First World War. She described the death of a close friend.

Dr Hout was able to see the cord connecting the physical and etheric bodies 'wound around through the room… as a curl of smoke'

Immediately after her heart had ceased to beat I distinctly saw something in appearance like smoke… ascend from her body… This form, shadowy at first, gradually changed and… resolved itself into a form like that of my friend, but glorified, with no trace on it of the spasm of pain which had seized her just before she died.

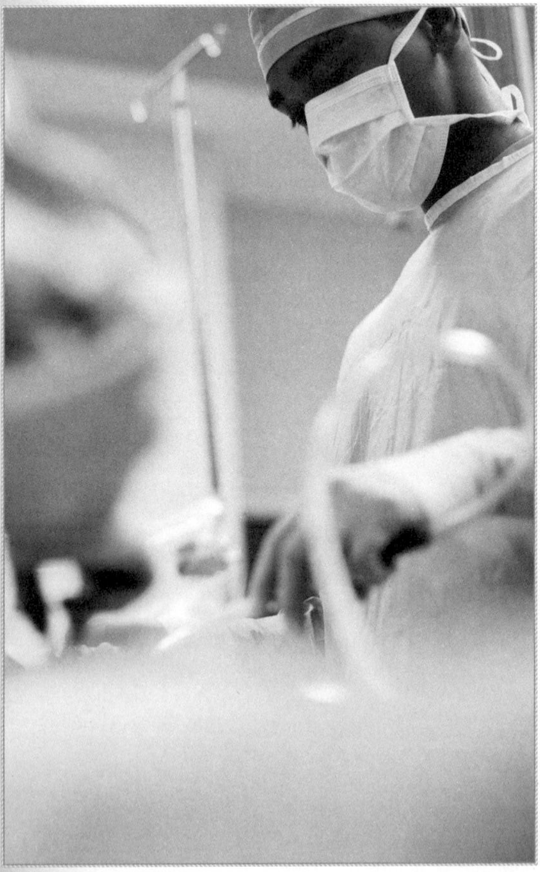

Perhaps even more convincing are the accounts of patients who have left their body under anaesthetic and have observed the procedures and heard the conversations of the medical staff while they were supposedly unconscious. In 1953 British surgeon George Sava published his memoirs, *A Surgeon Remembers*, in which he recalled the night he was called to revive Mrs Frances Gail, an elderly patient who had lapsed into a post-operative coma. His efforts were successful and when she recovered Mrs Gail casually remarked that during the procedure she had been outside her body and had heard and observed everything that had taken place in the operating theatre.

You didn't carry out the operation you first intended, did you, Mr Sava? You kept my body lying there under the anaesthetic while you and the others discussed whether it was strong enough to withstand what you proposed to do. You took away some pieces of bone. You were chiefly

> *troubled about the anaesthetic and told the anaesthetist, 'Do you think she can stand three hours of it? Heart all right?' The anaesthetist just nodded and said, 'She's okay especially considering she's no spring chicken.' Is that right?*

The surgeon had to admit that is exactly what happened.

The standard objection to the OBE phenomenon is that the individual concerned could have heard what was going on while they were unconscious and that all they did was to piece together the scene from snippets of conversation after their recovery. But in the case of Mrs Gail and many others who claim to have experienced an OBE, they were able to describe medical procedures as well as small but significant details they could only have seen from another viewpoint.

Sava concluded:

> *It is indeed a disquieting thought... that every time one operates, one's activities are under observation from the patient's astral body hovering overhead... a fascinating but frightening possibility.*

Even more remarkable is the incident involving a female patient whose astral body left the operating theatre because she was more 'curious' to know what her relatives were doing in the waiting room. She saw her husband anxiously pacing the corridor, but she couldn't see her daughter anywhere. The thought projected her to a local shop where her daughter was choosing a get well card. By looking over the girl's shoulder the mother was able to read the message in two of the cards then she saw her daughter put back the card with the more flippant message and pay for the other. When the daughter was finally allowed into the ward to visit her mother after the successful operation she was astonished to hear her recite the message of both the card she had bought and the one she had put back in the rack – all before she had given her mother the card.

The episode is just one of many thousands collected over many years by the tireless English researcher into the phenomenon, Dr Robert Crookall.

'It is a disquieting thought that one's activities are under observation from the patient's astral body, hovering overhead'

Celebrity Spirits

IN CASE ONE should be tempted to dismiss all such experiences as fantasies of the highly imaginative mind, it is worth noting that several celebrated pragmatists such as the hard-drinking American writer Ernest Hemingway have also admitted to having had similar experiences.

During World War One the young Hemingway was wounded by shrapnel from a mortar shell, at which point he felt his soul drawn out of his body.

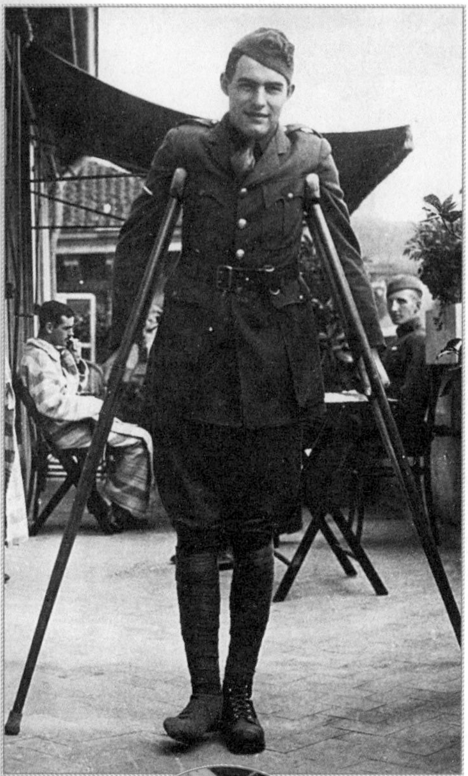

Hemingway [pictured left in 1918] compared the sensation to a silk handkerchief being whisked out of a pocket. For some minutes he was whirled around the battlefield before re-entering his body. The experience was dramatized in his wartime novel *A Farewell To Arms*:

> *I went out swiftly, all of myself and I knew I was dead and that it had all been a mistake to think you just died.*

Aviator Charles Lindbergh [below left] found it difficult to admit that he had experienced the phenomenon during his exhausting historic solo flight across the Atlantic in 1927. In 1977 he told a reporter:

> *I existed independently of time and matter. I felt myself departing from my body as I imagine a spirit would depart… But I remained connected to my body through a long extended strand, a strand so tenuous that it could have been severed by a breath… My visions are easily explained away through reason, but the longer I live the more limited I believe rationality to be.*

Many celebrities have talked openly of their out-of-body experiences and in doing so have helped bring the subject to greater public awareness. The American actress Shirley MacLaine was one of the first to actively publicize her paranormal experiences and as a result she became a spokesperson for the emerging New Age movement. However, her apparent willingness to believe that she had been an inhabitant of the legendary lost continent of Atlantis in a former incarnation has undermined her credibility in the minds of more serious researchers.

Actress Elizabeth Taylor was more reluctant to admit her out-of-body experiences, but eventually came

During surgery, Elizabeth Taylor felt herself leaving her body and being drawn through a tunnel towards a brilliant white light

round to believing that doing so might do more good than harm. She told talk show host Larry King that she had left her body during surgery and remembered being drawn through a tunnel towards a brilliant white light, common features of what are widely known as Near Death Experiences. She described being greeted by her third husband Michael Todd, who had been killed in a plane crash in 1958. He told her that she had to return, but she was very reluctant to do so because she was experiencing a state of bliss the like of which she had never known on earth. Then she was drawn back into her body and awoke to be told that she had been clinically dead.

> *I find it very hard to talk about, because it sounds so corny… they had given me up for dead and put my death notice on the wall. I shared this with the people that were in the room next to me. Then after that I told another group of friends, and I thought, 'Wow, this sounds really screwy. I think I'd better keep quiet about this.'*
>
> *For a long time I didn't talk about it, and it's still hard for me to talk about. But I have shared it with people with AIDS because if the moment occurs and you're really sharing, it's real. I am not afraid of death, because I have been there.*

In 1964 comic actor Peter Sellers shared a similar experience after suffering the first in a series of heart attacks. He too was declared clinically dead but at that moment all he could think about was how liberating it was to be free of his ailing body:

> *I just floated out of my physical form and I saw them cart my body away to the hospital. I went with it… I wasn't frightened… I was fine… it was my body that was in trouble… I saw an incredibly beautiful, bright, loving white light above me. I wanted to go to that white light more than anything. I've never wanted anything more. I know there was love, real love, on the*

Peter Sellers saw a hand reach through the light. He tried to touch it and hold on to it, so it would sweep him up and pull him through

> *other side of the light which was attracting me so much. It was kind and loving and I remember thinking, 'That's God.' Then I saw a hand reach through the light. I tried to touch it, to grab on to it, to clasp it so it could sweep me up and pull me through it.*

But then he heard a voice say, 'It's not time. Go back and finish. It's not time'. The experience haunted Sellers for the rest of his life, compounding the idea that life on earth was only temporary and not to be taken too seriously. It also sparked the thought that his talent for mimicry might be simply the ability to reawaken character traits and aspects of his personalities from his past lives.

He told his friend Shirley MacLaine:

I know I have lived many times before... that experience confirmed it to me, because in this lifetime I felt what it was for my soul to actually be out of my body. But ever since I came back, I don't know why I don't know what it is I'm supposed to do, or what I came back for.

Dallas actor Larry Hagman had an NDE in 1995 which profoundly affected his outlook on life and what might lie beyond it. Death, he believed, is...

just another stage of our development and that we go on to different levels of existence... This was not the end. There were more levels, an infinite number of levels, of existence, each one adding to the hum of the cosmic orchestra, as if we're always spiralling upward until we reach a state of atomic bliss...

A Near Birth Experience

IT HAS ALWAYS been assumed that discarnate spirits spend a certain time in a state between lives before reincarnating, but the following account related by a W. Martin of Liverpool, published in the *Sunday Express* in May 1935, suggests that the soul has some say in the matter:

In 1911, at the age of sixteen, I was staying about twelve miles away from my own home when a high wall was blown down by a sudden gust of wind as I was passing. A huge coping stone hit me on top of the head. It then seemed as if I could see myself lying on the ground, huddled up, with one corner of the stone resting on my head and quite a number of people rushing towards me. I watched them move the stone and someone took off his coat and put it under my head, and I heard all their comments: 'Fetch a doctor', 'His neck is broken', 'Skull smashed'.

One of the bystanders asked if anyone knew where I lived, and on being told I was lodging just around the corner, he instructed them to carry me there. All this time it appeared as though I were disembodied from the form lying on the ground and suspended in midair in the centre of the group, and I could hear everything that was being said.

As they started to carry me it was remarked that it would come as a blow to my people and I was immediately conscious of a desire to be with my mother. Instantly I was at home and father and mother were just sitting down to their mid-day meal.

The injured boy was conscious of a desire to be with his mother: 'Instantly I was at home and father and mother were sitting down to mid-day meal'

On my entrance mother sat bolt upright in her chair and said, 'Bert, something has happened to our boy.'

There followed an argument, but my mother refused to be pacified and said that if she caught the 2 pm train she would be with me before 3 pm. She had hardly left the room when there came a knock at the front door. It was a porter from the railway station with a telegram saying I was badly hurt.

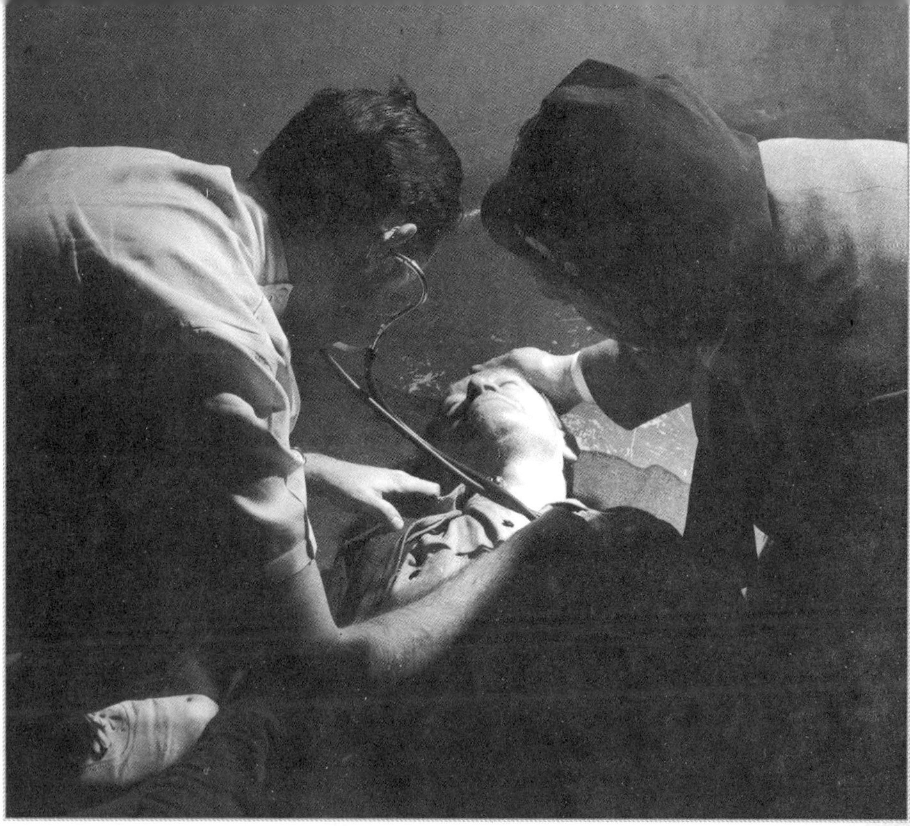

Then suddenly I was again transported – this time it seemed to be against my wish – to a bedroom, where a woman whom I recognized was in bed, and two other women were quietly bustling around, and a doctor was leaning over the bed. Then the doctor had a baby in his hands. At once I became aware of an almost irresistible impulse to press my face through the back of the baby's head so that my face would come out at the same place as the child's. The doctor said, 'It looks as though we have lost them both.' And again I felt the urge to take the baby's place to show him he was wrong, but the thought of my mother crying turned my thoughts in her direction, when straight away I was in a railway carriage with her and my father. I was still with them when they arrived at my lodgings and were shown to the room where I had been put to bed.

'All this time it appeared as though I were disembodied from the form lying on the ground and suspended in midair in the centre of the group'

Mother sat beside the bed and I longed to comfort her, and the realization came that I ought to do the same thing I felt impelled to do in the case of the baby and climb into the body on the bed. At last I succeeded, and the effort caused the real me to sit up in bed fully conscious. Mother made me lie down again, but I said I was all right, and remarked that it was odd that she knew that something was wrong before the porter had brought the telegram. Both she and dad were amazed at my knowledge… I said I had been close to birth as well as death, and told them that Mrs Wilson who lived close to us at home, had had a baby that day, but it was dead because I would not get into its body. We subsequently learnt that Mrs Wilson died on the same day at 2.05 pm after delivering a stillborn girl.

III
Lost Lives

Though I may not be a king in my future life, so much the better: I shall nevertheless live an active life and, on top of it, earn less ingratitude.

Frederick the Great

ONE OF THE ARGUMENTS voiced by those who do not believe in reincarnation and who scoff at those who claim to have recovered memories of their former lives, is that if there was a factual basis for these beliefs there would be records of similar stories dating back to ancient times. Why, they ask, have such stories only surfaced now, if they have been a fact of life and not merely a matter of faith? The truth is that there are numerous accounts of individuals from past centuries whose claims were so convincing that they were written down, but these are rarely cited by today's researchers because they prefer to offer cases that can be verified and supported by documentary evidence. Nevertheless, these early cases are worth examining if only to demonstrate that past life recollections are not a New Age fad or fantasy.

Village life: Fusa thought Katsugoro was playing a game when he asked her, at the age of seven, who she had been before she became his sister

✣ EARLY CASES ✣

Katsugoro

A TYPICAL CASE was that of Katsugoro, a young Japanese boy born on 10 October 1815, whose claim was thoroughly documented and the papers witnessed, sealed and then stored in the library of Count Sasaki in Tokyo for safekeeping. It was not until the end of the nineteenth century that they were unearthed and translated by a Western author, Lafcadio Hearn, while researching the customs and culture of the region for his book *Gleanings in Buddha Fields* (Houghton Mifflin, Boston, 1897).

Katsugoro lived in the village of Nakano Mura, with his father Genzo, his mother Sei and elder sister Fusa. When Katsugoro was seven he asked

Fusa who she had been before she became his sister. She naturally thought he was playing a new game and asked him the same question. But it was clear from his demeanour that he was not fantasizing, but recalling something that was as real to him as his present life. He said that his father had been called Kyubei and his mother was named Shidzu. They had lived in Hodokubo and his name at that time had been Tozo.

When Fusa later mentioned this incident to her grandmother, the old lady called Katsugoro to her side and asked him to tell her more. He added that he had been five years old when his father had died, and that he was then brought up by a man named Hanshiro who had moved into the family home. But he had no time to get to know his new father as at the age of six he had contracted smallpox and died shortly afterwards. Then he recalled seeing his lifeless body being placed in a jar and buried on a hill as was the custom at the time.

The next thing he recalled was being brought to Genzo's house by an old man who told him, 'Now you must be reborn, for it is three years since you died. You are to be reborn in this house.'

For three days his spirit lingered in the house. 'Then I entered mother's honourable womb… I remember that I was born without any pain at all!'

Intrigued by her grandson's story, the old woman offered to take him to Hodokubo to find the tomb of Kyubei his father. And when they reached the village, the boy pulled away from his grandmother and ran to a house crying 'This is the house'. Before she could stop him Katsugoro had run inside. His grandmother followed, excusing her grandson's intrusion and finding herself having to explain the whole business to the occupants. But no apology was necessary because it turned out that the owners were Hanshiro and his wife Shidzu, who were able to confirm that they had once had a son, Tozo, who had died thirteen years earlier of smallpox at the age of six.

Those were not the only verifiable facts. His real father had been Kyubei, as the boy had claimed, but even more incredible was the fact that Katsugoro began to identify landmarks that he recognized from his former life and also singled out properties that had not been built at the time of his 'death'. This was enough to satisfy Hanshiro and Shidzu who willingly signed affidavits to this effect, which were considered of such significance that they were entrusted to the library of Count Sasaki.

Alexandrina Samona

ANOTHER early example is that of Alexandrina Samona, whose case must be unique in the history of reincarnation in that the disembodied spirit of the deceased was said to have announced her own rebirth.

On 15 March 1910, five-year-old Alexandrina Samona died in Palermo, Sicily, of meningitis despite the best efforts of her father, Carmelo, to save her. Carmelo Samona was a respected physician, but his rational, scientific view of the world would be shattered by subsequent events.

Several days after the death of her daughter, Dr Samona's wife Adela dreamt that the child had appeared to her and said, 'Mother, do not cry any more. I have not left you; I have only gone a little away. Look, I shall become little, like this', at which the little girl showed her mother the likeness of a new-born baby.

Then she added, 'You are therefore going to have to begin to suffer again on account of me.' Three days later, the mother had the same dream.

The logical explanation for the dreams would be that Adela was unconsciously compensating for her loss by wishing for another child to replace her, but there are two factors which contradict this. The first is that the mother did not believe in reincarnation and the second is that she had recently undergone an operation which made it physically impossible for her to bear any more children.

'Mother, do not cry any more. I have not left you; I have only gone a little away'

The dreams did not, however, lessen the grief and several days later while Adela was in an extreme state of distress she and her husband heard three loud bangs in their apartment. Suspecting that it might be their daughter attempting to communicate, and desperate to try anything that might help them, they decided to hold a series of séances. Two apparitions manifested themselves at the first of these: one was Alexandrina and the other identified itself as an aunt of hers who had died some years before. Alexandrina's spirit confirmed that she had been responsible for the three loud knocks and had indeed appeared in her mother's dreams in order to alleviate her suffering and to reassure her that she would be reborn before Christmas of that year together with a twin sister.

If that was all there was to the case it would have been filed away in the archives of the Society for Psychical Research, who were investigating numerous incidents of this kind at the turn of the century. But there was more to it than that. Much more.

On 22 November 1910, Adela Samona gave birth to twin daughters, one of whom so closely resembled Alexandrina that her parents named her after the dead girl. She had hyperaemia of the left eye, as had her namesake, a peculiar condition of the right ear known as seborrhea, and strikingly similar facial asymmetry. Also, she happened to be left-handed like her dead sister. In the following months and years it was noted that the two Alexandrinas bore more than a passing physical resemblance to each other. Alexandrina II was solitary, excessively tidy and passive. She insisted that her hands were clean and, most curiously, she shared the first Alexandrina's fierce dislike of cheese. These traits had to be more than merely genetic because the other twin was of a different physical type and possessed a

Alexandrina told her parents she had been to Monreale before, even though it was her dead sister who had actually met 'the lady with horns'

markedly different disposition – she was active, alert and outgoing.

Her father later told the *Journal of the American Society for Psychical Research* (April and July 1960): 'I can affirm in the most positive manner that in every way, except for the hair and eyes, which are actually a little lighter than those of the first Alexandrina at the same age, the resemblance continues to be perfect. But even more than on the physical side, the psychological similarity developing in the child gives the case further and greater interest.'

By the age of ten there were more disquieting aspects for the parents to ponder upon. When the girls were informed that a holiday to Monreale was planned, Alexandrina let them know that she had been there before (which was not the case) and that she recalled being in the company of 'a lady who had horns', which her mother understood to be a reference to a lady who had disfiguring wens on her head. But it was not Alexandrina who had seen this woman but her dead namesake. When the girl began to describe the local sites, and even the colour of the robes worn by the priests whom she had seen there, her mother knew it was time to have her claims investigated.

Fortunately, Dr Samona had mentioned the prophetic dreams and the prediction of the miraculous twin birth to a priest and several family members before the girls were born and so the couple were able to locate several witnesses who could corroborate their story. Their statements were published in the Italian periodical *Filosofia della Scienza* and the French *Journal du Magnetisme,* which ensured they became the talk of their day. The case also featured in two seminal studies of the subject of reincarnation – Dr. Charles Lancelin's book, *La Vie Posthume* (Published by Henri Durville, Paris, *c.*1920) pp. 309–363 and A. de Rochas' *Les Vies Successives, Chacornac,* Paris 1911, pp. 338–45 (publisher unknown), proving that such stories are not as new as many people may think.

Blanche Battista

AN UNCANNILY SIMILAR case, dating to 1906, was recounted by an unimpeachable source, the Reverend Leslie Weatherhead, president of the Methodist Conference of Great Britain, during a talk given in 1957 entitled 'The Case for Reincarnation'.

'In the fourth month of the pregnancy, she had a strange waking dream… Blanche said, "Mother, I am coming back."'

Captain and Mrs Battista, Italians, had a little daughter, born in Rome, whom they called Blanche. To help look after this child they employed a French-speaking Swiss 'nanny' called Mary. Mary taught her little charge to sing in French a lullaby song. Blanche grew very fond of this song and it was sung to her repeatedly. Unfortunately Blanche died and Mary returned to Switzerland.

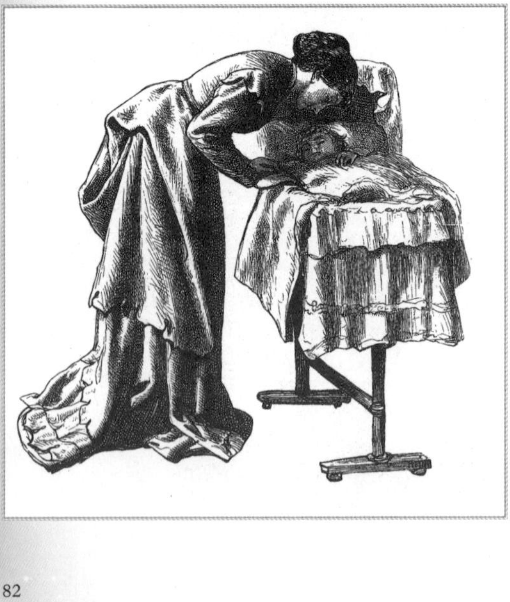

Captain Battista writes, 'The cradle song which would have recalled to us only too painful memories of our deceased child, ceased absolutely to be heard in the house… all recollection of [it] completely escaped from our minds.'

Three years after the death of Blanche, the mother, Signora Battista, became pregnant, and in the fourth month of the pregnancy she had a strange waking dream. She insists that she was wide awake when Blanche appeared to her again and said to her in her old familiar voice, 'Mother, I am coming back.' The vision then melted away. Captain Battista was sceptical, but when the new baby was born in February, 1906, he acquiesced to her being also given the name Blanche. The new Blanche resembled the old in every possible way.

Nine years after the death of the first Blanche, when the second was about six years of age, an extraordinary thing happened. I will use Captain Battista's own words. 'While I was with my wife in my study which adjoins our bedroom, we heard, both of us, like a distant echo, the famous cradle song, and the voice came from the bedroom where we had left our little daughter Blanche fast asleep... We found the child sitting up on the bed and singing with an excellent French accent the cradle song which neither of us had certainly ever taught her. My wife... asked her what it was she was singing, and the child, with the utmost promptitude, answered that she was singing a French song... "Who, pray, taught you this pretty song?" I asked her. "Nobody. I know it out of my own head," answered the child...'

The Captain ends with a sentence which, short of calling him a liar, it is hard to set on one side. 'The reader may draw any conclusion he likes from this faithful narrative of facts to which I bear my personal witness. For myself, the conclusion I draw from them is that... the dead are permitted to visit the world again in another body.'

Truth is Stranger than Fiction

UNTIL VERY RECENTLY reincarnation was practically a taboo subject in the West. The people who accepted it as a fact of life were likely to be members of the spiritualist churches and esoteric societies such as the Theosophists and Rudolf Steiner's anthropological movement. Talk of past lives outside these circles was likely to be taken as the first sign of senility or at best, eccentricity.

The novelist Joan Grant was fortunate in having a husband who took her claims seriously and who encouraged her to draw on her recollections as the basis for a series of historical novels set in ancient Egypt. The first of these, *Winged Pharaoh*, centred on the story of Sekeeta, a princess in the third millennium BC and was reputedly written without the benefit of research of any kind. On its publication in 1937 it was greeted with great critical acclaim by academics who praised its historical accuracy. They were less enamoured, however, of its author's claim to have been Sekeeta in a previous lifetime, but despite the derision which her claims invited and the obvious embarrassment of her family, Grant stuck by

her story and eventually wrote her autobiography in which she set out to justify her assertion.

During the last 20 years seven books of mine have been published as historical novels which to me are biographies of previous lives I have known. I was twenty-nine before I managed to recover the technique of being able to live an earlier incarnation in detail and as a deliberate exercise. Until then, my conviction that I had had many lifetimes... was based on disjointed episodes from seven previous lives; four male and three female. These memories, although as natural as memories from more immediate yesterdays, are frustrating because I could not fill in the gaps in continuity which would have linked them into coherent sequences. That everyone else did not have even this small degree of Far Memory was so difficult to understand that until I was eleven I presumed that other people's reticence about their own Long History was only another incomprehensible taboo which complicated an Edwardian childhood...

Despite her inner conviction Joan was nevertheless troubled by doubts and not afraid to confront them.

I was always alert to the possibility that the incidents of Far Memory might be fantasies based on my own hopes and fears, or on what I had heard or seen or read. Had radio, television or a more primitive form of cinematography been invented my self doubts would have been even more acute. With practice I learned how to discriminate between the pseudo and the factual... the emotions and the sensations associated with a genuine recall were as vivid as though they were being felt by myself in the factual present. The alteration of the focus of my attention again caused an incident in the past to become the Here and Now. Sometimes this could be not only terrifying but also physically painful... So far as I have been able to discover it is no more difficult to recall an episode which took place several millennia ago than to recall one from the current or preceding century.

Joan makes the analogy between the human personality and an orange which appears to the eye to be a single object, but when the skin is peeled back each segment can be seen as a different facet of the whole. The analogy of the orange is also relevant for grasping the concept of Time as being an illusion which prevents us from accepting that reincarnation is a natural process. Time, she argues, is comparable to the centre of the orange to which the separate segments are equidistant and not like a chain on which are strung a series of beads.

Opposite: author Joan Grant claimed a previous life as an Egyptian princess named Sekeeta

Joan Grant's first visit to Egypt produced a sense of sadness that so little remained from the time of her previous life

Curiously, her first visit to Egypt in March 1935 did not trigger a vivid flashback, but only a sense of sadness that so little of the impressive monuments, palaces and temples remained. Eighteen months later, while experimenting with psychometry on a scarab (deriving impressions from inanimate objects), she stimulated the first of over 115 total recalls which formed the basis of her 120,000-word debut novel. She had dictated much of it to her husband, a respected psychiatrist, while in a light hypnotic trance, but initially she spoke at such speed that he was unable to record more than a handful of furiously scribbled notes. She had to persuade her husband to instruct her former self to speak more clearly and at a reasonable pace or risk losing the details which brought the tale so vividly to life.

The other problem was that there was no way of determining which moment in Sekeeta's life Joan was going to relive during a session. She might find herself recalling a family festivity or observing a traumatic incident from the princess' past, such as the time she observed a crude surgical operation in which a man's skull was being trepanned after an accident with an overturned chariot.

It is interesting that in trance Joan/Sekeeta reaffirms the belief that the Egyptian magical rituals were used to initiate selected individuals into the mysteries of life and death, specifically the practice of soul travel, or astral projection. The initiate was sealed for several days and nights within a narrow chamber designed to replicate a tomb. This primitive sensory deprivation experiment would serve as a rite of passage into spiritual awareness and the initiate would hopefully emerge reborn.

✣ Speaking in Tongues ✣

XENOGLOSSY IS THE clinical term for the ability to speak foreign languages that one has not consciously learnt. In many cases this amounts to no more than a few phrases and is explained by the fact that the subject has unconsciously retained a memory of hearing or seeing these foreign phrases in their past. However, this plausible theory cannot explain the rare instances in which individuals have spoken at length in an ancient language and responded to questions in an archaic tongue. The question it raises is whether such incidents are examples of past life recall, some form of spirit communication, or as psychologists believe, the result of a fragmenting of the psyche into separate sub-personalities, each with their own distinctive characteristics and identity. A more fanciful explanation is that the messages are being 'channelled' by discarnate entities, but if that were so it seems more likely that they would communicate in the medium's own language rather than risk losing the gist of their message in translation.

'The spirit's name was Nona and she began to communicate in her mother tongue'

The most famous case of this kind was the so-called Rosemary case, which came to public awareness in 1928 after a young English woman had begun to produce automatic writing. The phenomenon involves the writing of intelligible prose at a faster speed than it would be possible to consciously construct the sentences. Rosemary (whose surname was withheld) initially consulted a doctor with an interest in psychic phenomena. Dr Wood encouraged her to attend séances where she would act as a medium for the spirits he assumed would wish to communicate through her.

One of these spirits identified itself as a former friend of Rosemary from an earlier incarnation. The spirit's name was Nona and she had known Rosemary in ancient Egypt. Such claims would have invited derision from every serious psychic researcher were it not for the fact that 'Nona' began to communicate in her mother tongue with the good doctor and he recorded these conversations phonetically for future verification. After some considerable time Dr Wood decided to take his notes to an acknowledged expert in ancient languages, who confirmed that the phrases were authentic and that they were credible responses to the doctor's questions.

During the course of several years, approximately 5,000 words and phrases were communicated in trance through Rosemary and these were subsequently verified as being genuine examples of the ancient Egyptian language. Moreover, her pronunciation was consistent, a feat which would not be possible if they were random utterings.

A Child's Tale

IN APRIL 1932 the Hollywood actor Melvyn Douglas related an anecdote to *Modern Screen* magazine concerning a mother and child of his acquaintance, which must qualify as one of the first cases of its kind to receive publicity in the West.

Publicity shot of Melvyn Douglas who won two Oscars, a Tony and an Emmy. He was intrigued by the strange utterings of the boy

Robin Hull was a little fellow, just five years old. He talked well for his age, for the most part. But often… his mother noticed him uttering strange sounds… they were, she decided, an unintelligible abracadabra left over from his infancy. However, as time went on and Robin came to speak more and more fluently, she really thought it odd that he should continue uttering these same strange sounds…

'I really don't understand it,' she told her dinner guests one evening. 'Robin really says these sounds as if they had definite meaning to him. Moreover, he repeats many of them so frequently that I have come to recognize them.' One of the Hull guests was a woman interested in reincarnation. 'Would you let me come and sit with you in the nursery one afternoon… just on the chance Robin might talk this way?' she asked.

'I'd be glad to,' Mrs Hull told her. So the next afternoon found the two women in the nursery with master Hull. He was extremely obliging. He said dozens of strange-sounding words. His mother's guest was fascinated.

'I'm sure he is saying real words,' she said. 'Words which would mean something to someone… if we could only find the right someone… Please let me bring a professor I know… He is familiar with a number of the Asiatic languages.'

Mrs Hull agreed to have the professor come, although… she didn't relish a lot of people with strange beliefs trooping into his nursery and proceeding to read their own meaning into everything he said. A week later her friend came with the professor… Robin… talked as usual. He very evidently wasn't at all self-conscious about these strange sounds he made… Finally, the professor turned to Mrs Hull.

'The words Robin keeps saying are from a language and dialect used in Northern Tibet,' he told her. 'There's no doubt about many of them. Others I do not recognize at all… Was he, by any remote chance, there as a baby? Have you or your husband, or any of your family, or any of your husband's family ever been there?' To all these questions Alice Hull shook her head. Then the professor called Robin… 'Where did you learn the words you say?' 'In school,' Robin told him. 'But, Robin dear,' interrupted his mother, 'you've never been to school.' 'When I went to school – before,' said Robin, his little brow furrowed. 'Do you remember what the school looked like?' the professor asked…

'The words Robin keeps saying are from a language and dialect used in Northern Tibet'

For a long minute Robin was thoughtful. Then he said, 'Yes, I remember. It was in the mountains. But they weren't the kind of mountains we went to in the summer, Mama… ' 'Was this school you went to made of wood or of stone…?' 'It was stone,' said Robin. 'And tell me, what were the teachers like? Were they ladies or were they men?' 'They were men,' Robin showed no hesitancy on this score. 'But they didn't dress like you and my daddy. They had skirts. With a sash around their waist that looked like a robe… ' And Robin gave a detailed description of the school.

The professor was so impressed with everything the boy said, he undertook the long journey to Asia and Northern Tibet in search of the school. Fortunately, the latter area is close to China and not so difficult to access as Eastern Tibet. Eventually the Hulls received this letter from him.

'I have found the school about which Robin told us. It is in the Kuen-lun mountains, rocky and arid, and, of course, not at all like the mountains

where Robin spends his summers. And it tallies with Robin's description in every detail. So do the lamas [priests] who teach there.'

In 1966 Dr Ian Stevenson, Professor of Psychiatry at the University of Virginia, published the findings of a long and thorough investigation into a similar case, in an article which became the basis of his highly influential study *Twenty Cases Suggestive of Reincarnation.*

The subject was the wife of a Philadelphia doctor who had agreed to be hypnotically regressed by her husband. It is assumed that the doctor expected to regress his wife to her childhood to reveal the source of a fear or phobia, but in the event she re-experienced her death in a former life. She felt a blow to her head and had the sensation that she was drowning. When the initial shock had subsided she informed her husband in broken English that she was a man by the name of Jensen Jacoby. Her accent was unfamiliar to the doctor but he later learnt that it was Swedish. In due course sessions were arranged to which native Swedish speakers were invited. After the doctor had put his wife in a trance she would answer questions in Swedish from the guests, who translated for the doctor's benefit.

The school in the Kuen-lun mountains matched Robin's description in every detail, down to the lamas who taught there

What intrigued Dr Stevenson was the fact that the wife used words and phrases that had not been used by her interrogators. Many of them were the names of seventeenth century objects that only a historian would have known.

✣ Group Souls ✣

IT IS SAID that for every soul there is a counterpart, a twin or soul mate, and that each of us belong to a group soul – a family of compatible individuals who reincarnate together over many lifetimes. Roles are exchanged with each incarnation so that we may all experience what it is like to be a father, a mother, a son, a daughter, a brother and so on and grow through the give and take that characterizes a real relationship. This belief is thought to account for the bond between particularly close friends and for that rare feeling that you may have experienced when you meet someone for the first time and feel that you know them already.

However, it is extremely rare for the individuals within a group soul to become conscious of their karmic connection. The members of one such group were made aware of their relationship under very remarkable circumstances. It began with a young schoolgirl's nightmares: she dreamt she was being burned to death as a heretic in thirteenth-century France. In 1944, at the age of twelve, she wrote a graphic account of her final moments.

> *The pain was maddening. You should pray to God when you're dying, if you can pray when you're in agony. In my dream I didn't pray to God… I didn't know when you were burnt to death you'd bleed. I thought the blood would all dry up in the terrible heat. But I was bleeding heavily. The blood was dripping and hissing in the flames. I wished I had enough blood to put the flames out. The worst part was my eyes. I hate the thought of going blind… In this dream I was going blind. I tried to close my eyelids, but I couldn't. They must have been burnt off…*

A schoolgirl dreamt about being burnt to death as a heretic in thirteenth-century France and wrote a graphic account of the agony

Martyrs of Montségur

FOR MANY YEARS she continued to suffer from violent nightmares in which she dreamt she was being persecuted with other members of her sect. She was still experiencing the nightmares after her marriage and her husband eventually persuaded her to see a psychiatrist. She was referred to Dr Arthur Guirdham, who at that time (1961) was the chief psychiatrist at Bath Hospital in England. After a thorough examination he declared that

The expulsion of 'the heretics' from Carcasonne: in the 1960s, a woman suffered from violent nightmares arising from these distant events

she was perfectly sane and not exhibiting any signs of neuroses.

But she continued to be treated by Guirdham for the recurrent nightmares and evidently felt sufficiently confident in his abilities to confide in him a secret she had kept for decades. While still a schoolgirl she had kept a journal. In it she had noted names and dates and had given a full description of everything that had transpired in her dreams as well as the thoughts and impressions that had come to mind during the course of her waking hours. She had suspected that more had been involved than fear or fantasy. The same personalities appeared in successive dreams and the location was always the same. She had even described customs, costumes, coins and jewellery and had drawn a map of the town in which she had lived and had been imprisoned. The most intriguing items, however, were the verses she had written in Medieval French, a language she had never studied.

Dr Guirdham obtained copies of the notes from his patient who, incidentally, remains anonymous to this day, and sent them to scholars for authentification. Professor Pere Nelli of Toulouse University immediately wrote back to say that he was satisfied that the girl had accurately described the sacred rituals of the Cathars, a heretical Christian sect who had been massacred at Montségur in the French Pyrenees in 1243. Further research helped to identify several of the personalities she had described, even though they were minor officials that would not have been included in a general history of the period. Fortunately, the diligent scribes of the Inquisition had kept impeccable notes, which were available for consultation.

Dr Guirdham was not a believer in reincarnation and has since stated that he had not even considered the possibility that this might be a possible explanation. He was then working on the assumption that it was a psychological phenomenon. But the devil, as they say, was in the detail. The woman had described being held prisoner in the crypt of a church and she named the church. The considered opinion of the experts was that captured heretics would never have been kept in a church, but further research unearthed the fact that on this occasion so many of them were arrested that their captors had no choice but to use the crypt.

Intrigued, Guirdham made the journey to the South of France and there consulted manuscripts which were not available to the public. Here he was able to confirm many small but significant details pertaining to his patient's description of Cathar costumes and customs as well as four of the songs she had noted down. They were correct word for word.

Dr Guirdham also suffered from recurring nightmares which ended after meeting the woman. Could they both have been martyrs of Montségur?

But this was not the most intriguing aspect of the case. Apparently Dr Guirdham had also suffered from recurring nightmares, which always began in the same way – with a figure entering a room in which he was imprisoned. These dreams ended after Dr Guirdham's first meeting with

the woman who appears to have been a Cathar martyr, the implication being that they had both been members of the same sect and that their resolve to face their memories was sufficient to put their fears to rest.

Dr Guirdham subsequently came into contact with a further eight individuals who were able, under regression, to recall a former life as a Cathar. The curious circumstances under which he met these individuals convinced Dr Guirdham of the existence of soul groups. In this instance they were evidently predestined to meet again in order to resolve issues which had arisen from their relationship and their actions seven centuries earlier. If this is true, it raises the question of why they did not reincarnate as a group earlier than this – or had they done so and for one reason or another failed to settle their unfinished business?

The first of the further eight subjects was an RAF officer who confessed that he had once climbed Montségur and had been overcome with a feeling of nausea and a belief that the site was bathed in blood. He had not known of its history at the time.

Under Dr Guirdham's supervision the group underwent collective regression sessions that revealed further instances of their life together, including obscure details that contradicted the official records of the period, but which were later confirmed by experts. Professor Duvernoy of Toulouse expressed his astonishment at Guirdham's detailed knowledge of Catharism and when told how he had obtained this information the professor was keener than ever to contribute to the investigation.

Summing up his findings in a lecture to the College of Psychic Science in 1969, Dr Guirdham commented:

> *If the professors at Toulouse are amazed at the accuracy with which an English girl can produce details of Catharism known to few, that is good enough for me… All I have done in this matter was to listen to the story, act as an amateur historian and to verify from many sources the details she had noted. I believe this to be a unique and entirely valid experience.*

• Déjà Vu •

MANY OF US have, at one time or another, felt that a particular place is strangely familiar, even though we have not been there before. Could it be that we were here in a previous life, we wonder? Or is it possible that we are experiencing *déjà vu* (literally, 'already seen'), a phenomenon, which psychologists believe is caused by the split second time discrepancy that

A sea of faces: English troops on their way to Arras during the First World War

occurs when the brain receives two separate signals from the retina? Such a mundane explanation might account for the relatively vague feelings of familiarity, but it cannot explain the numerous instances in which individuals have accurately described locations that they have never visited.

Swedish psychiatrist Nils Jacobson featured the following case in his book *Life Without Death*? (1974). One of Jacobson's male patients had complained of having trance-like visions in which he had been a soldier in the First World War. He saw a scene at a railway station through the soldier's eyes as he bade farewell to the girl he loved. He called her Catherine and she wept as she said goodbye to her Marcel. He experienced the journey that followed in a state similar to those who describe out-of-body-experiences or lucid dreams.

‘A male patient had complained of having trance-like visions in which he had been a soldier in the First World War’

But this was no ordinary dream. The train finally arrived at Arras, then the troops disembarked and marched to the front line. In the next ‘scene’ his battalion was assaulting a village, but he never reached it. He felt a blow, then a burning pain in his chest, and everything went black.

The visions had occurred several times, but it was only when the man found himself temptingly close to Arras during a family holiday that he finally decided to see if the landscape he had seen in his visions was real or imagined.

At first the countryside was unfamiliar but then he came to the outskirts of Bapaume and it was as if he was walking through a waking dream. He led his bemused family through the winding lanes to the edge of a field from which could be seen the village where he had been killed. But on entering the village nothing was recognizable. Every feature had been clear and distinct in his visions, but this was not the same village. Fortunately his son spoke reasonable French and was keen to get to the bottom of the matter.

He engaged the locals in conversation and discovered that the entire village had been shelled into rubble during the First World War and had been rebuilt in the 1930s. Photographs were obtained which showed that the church and other landmarks had originally been exactly as the man had described.

A similar experience is recorded in Guy Playfair's *The Indefinite Boundary*. Playfair, an English psychical researcher, lived in Brazil for several years. During that time he investigated the story of a middle-aged lady who had been plagued by violent recurring dreams of an explicitly sexual nature since early childhood, when she was too young to understand what she was experiencing.

In later life she visited Pompeii and there recognized the scene of her dreams. She led her travelling companions unhesitatingly to the house in which she claimed she had once lived and where the events of the dreams had originally taken place. It was a brothel.

• Physical Clues •

THE MYSTICALLY MINDED have always believed that physical disorders are often symptomatic of dis-ease in the psyche and that many chronic complaints can be cured by addressing the issues they symbolize. For example, someone who feels they are carrying too much responsibility may develop pains in their lower back as if they have been bearing a heavy burden; someone who fears they cannot escape a situation may manifest stiffness or ulcers in their legs; and someone who believes that no one listens to them may develop throat or speech problems. Psychotherapists have long suspected a connection between a patient's mental state and their physical wellbeing and now even general medical professionals are beginning to acknowledge that there is often a direct link between the two. However, the problem with treating psychosomatic conditions by using panaceas is that the relief is often only temporary. Empathy only goes so far, especially if the source of the disorder or disease is in a past life.

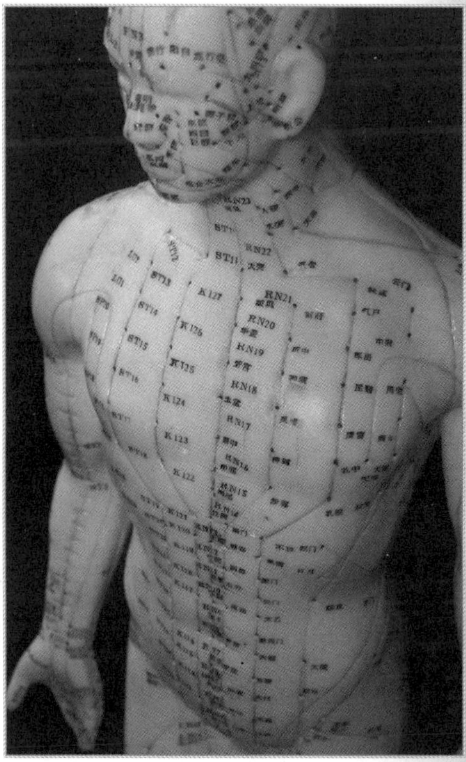

In recent years, Chinese acupuncture and other 'alternative therapies' have gained acceptance in the West

Old school occultist Alice Bailey identified the karmic clues to serious illness as early as 1953, but her book *Esoteric Healing* (Lucis Press, 1972) was not read outside esoteric circles. It was not until the late 1970s, when psychotherapist Morris Netherton documented a series of cases suggesting that heart disease and cancer might be manifestations of trauma, that the subject was given serious consideration by the more open-minded members of the medical profession.

While using deep breathing techniques to help a woman client through the trauma following a hysterectomy, regression therapist Roger Woolger awakened within her the memory of a primitive past-life sacrifice, where her belly was being ripped open. On another occasion, while working with a young man who had had several serious knee operations following a skiing accident, Woolger uncovered a life in which the young man had lost a leg beneath that same knee in battle.

Two other serious incidents of a similar nature had occurred in former incarnations.

Theoretically, such incidents can leave a psychic residue or weakness in the etheric double, which will mean that this area of the body will be prone to problems in subsequent lives if the patient is not treated. Treatment involves identifying the incident which was the source of the problem using regression, psychodrama, bioenergetic exercises or bodywork. Psychodrama is simply the re-enactment of the original incident. Bodywork requires the patient or a spiritual healer to scan for cold spots indicating breaks or blockages in the etheric body. Healing can then be given at a psychic level to repair tears and stimulate the *chakras*, the subtle energy centres located in the forehead, throat, heart, solar plexus, abdomen, groin and legs, so that the energy can flow freely through the network of vein-like meridian lines that connect them.

Despite previous scepticism, Western doctors now accept acupuncture points have distinct effects on cerebral activity governing specific body areas

This might sound fantastic to those who put their faith in conventional medicine, but it is the basis of many ancient medical systems, all of which have effected seemingly miraculous cures without the side-effects associated with pharmaceutical drugs.

These systems include Chinese acupuncture and other 'alternative' therapies originating in the East, such as reflexology.

In *Other Lives, Other Selves* (1986), Woolger describes facilitating a cathartic release of pain from a woman client who was suffering from lupus and attendant arthritic-like pain in her joints, by guiding her through a

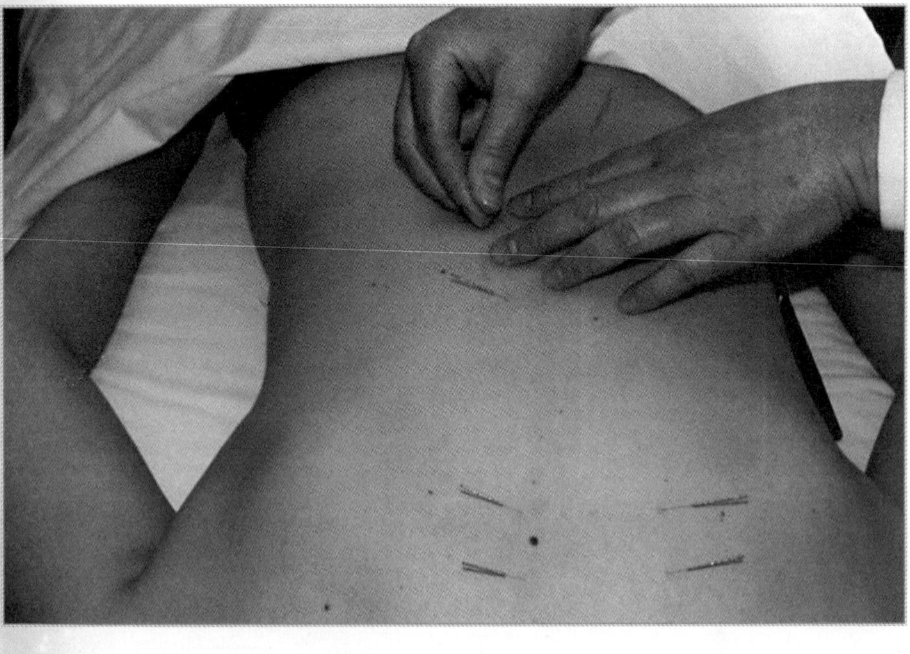

repressed memory of a previous life in which she had been dismembered in a bomb explosion. The shock of the explosion, and the trauma of seeing her mutilated body as she left it, had imprinted on her psyche the dying thought, 'I'll never use my legs and arms again!'.

Other symptoms, it is thought, might be self-imposed, in that some sufferers might have taken on their disability or disorder in order to learn compassion and clear their karmic debt to others. This does not, of course, mean that all disabled people are guilty, or believe themselves guilty of an offence in a past life and are punishing themselves – only that some might be doing so – and it is only a theory to which the majority of therapists do not subscribe.

Another of Woolger's female patients, who suffered from severe arthritis in her legs and arms, recalled a past life in which she had been a Roman commander who had crucified whole villages of rebellious Gauls, but who had died with the realization of the suffering he had caused. In such cases bodywork and psychodrama would be ineffective. Only the heartfelt expression of remorse and the need to be forgiven would initiate healing. Woolger wrote that:

A female patient recalled a past life in which she had been a Roman commander who had crucified whole villages of rebellious Gauls

> *Often, when a crucial story is released from the etheric or bioplasma body, there will be extraordinary discharges of subtle energy in the form of shaking, vomiting, tingling, hot and cold flushes, vibrating, and even the release of strange odors from the body. Such movements of energy, called kriyas in Yoga and 'streaming', in Reichian work, are little understood by Western science but are all part of the rebalancing of the subtle energy system at the etheric level.*

Much more complex, and therefore somewhat harder to work with, are cases where the past-life residues in the emotional body penetrate and deform the etheric system or the bioplasma and, with it, the physical body. These are the clients who somaticize their emotional problems, carrying them, as it were, in different parts of the body.

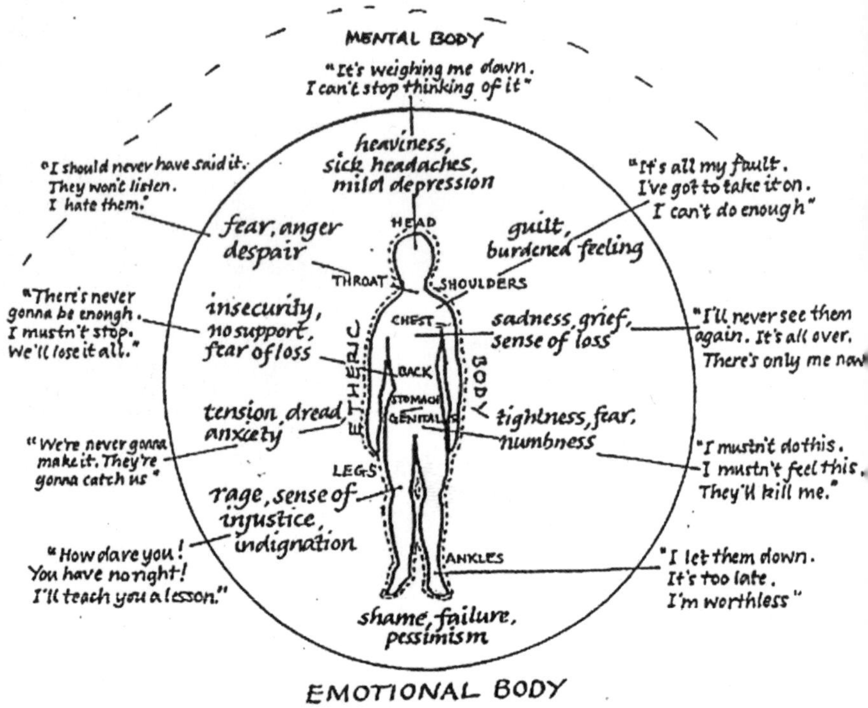

The diagram illustrates how the etheric/bioplasma and the physical systems might be afflicted by past-life trauma. [Reprinted courtesy of Roger Woolger.]

TYPICAL SYMPTOMS

Eyes Recurrent eye infections and psychosomatic glaucoma could be symptomatic of problems of perception. You might have witnessed something so horrific in a former life that you might have willed yourself to be blind to injustice or brutality in the next.

Ears Recurrent ear infections and a reluctance to react when other people talk to you can indicate an unconscious desire to ignore what you do not want to acknowledge. Effectively 'turning a deaf ear' to the facts which may have originated in a former life when you were falsely accused of something such as heresy or witchcraft perhaps.

Head Migraines can be symptomatic of an unwillingness to acknowledge an unpleasant experience or could be a reaction to pressure.

Mouth Persistent mouth ulcers and a dry mouth when trying to speak suggests problems in a past life with self-esteem and self-expression. In extreme cases it can be self-inflicted to atone for having falsely accused someone in a former life.

Nose and throat Sinus problems and persistent sore throats can be indicative of a death by drowning, suffocation or strangulation.

Neck, shoulders and back Aches and pains in these areas can indicate a reluctance to bear a burden or take on more than your fair share of responsibility. The most common source is a former life in which the person had to raise a family by themselves.

Stomach Digestive disorders can be attributed to suppressed emotions such as bitterness, resentment and anger. In the most serious cases this dis-ease of the soul can manifest as cancer in the physical body as the unprocessed emotional energy poisons the cells.

Skin The most common form of skin ailment is eczema which can be symptomatic of the need to 'get out of one's skin', either because the person is uncomfortable being themselves or because they feel acutely vulnerable. An experienced therapist will be able to identify whether the source of the problem lies in the present or the past.

Genitals Impotence, frigidity and lack of bladder control could be attributable to guilt or fear created by a trauma such as rape in a past life.

Legs and Feet Stiffness, swollen ankles, leg ulcers and other ailments of the lower limbs are likely to be manifestations of the need to escape, to run away which conflicts with the knowledge that this is impractical or impossible. If the source does not originate in the present, it could be traced back to a former life in which the individual was imprisoned or denied the opportunity to leave their home because they had commitments or obligations.

Hands Arthritis and clumsiness can manifest in order to express the fear of not being able to hold on to something of value. In a previous life you may have suffered a traumatic bereavement such as the loss of a child, enforced separation or the loss of status, self-respect or precious possessions.

Sylvia Gainsford was haunted by a dream of being shot in battle. She would wake with a real pain where the bullet had entered

Psychic artist Sylvia Gainsford, illustrator of *The Tarot of The Old Path* and my own *Kabbalah Cards*, was haunted by a recurring dream during her childhood which appears to have been a clue to a former life.

> *In the dream I was in the midst of a terrible battle. It was fierce hand to hand combat and I was so frightened that I fled the field. It was so vivid and real, it wasn't like a dream at all. I remember being afraid for my*

life and running until I couldn't run any longer. Then I stumbled and fell. I lay still for a while hoping that the enemy would walk by thinking that I was dead but the next moment I was shot in the back and awoke in a cold sweat with a real pain where the bullet had entered. It took a few moments for that feeling to fade. Later in life I had serious kidney problems which is where the bullet would have lodged and I have always believed that it was guilt that brought this on. I was punishing myself for having abandoned my comrades.

'A six-year-old Indian boy insisted he had been beheaded in his previous life by a jealous relative'

Birthmarks

THOSE WHO DISMISS the idea of reincarnation, on the grounds that there is no hard scientific proof to support it, cannot have considered the many recorded incidents of karmic birthmarks. This bizarre phenomenon in which birthmarks appear to take the form of scars is thought to be the physical manifestation of fatal injuries that occurred in the individual's previous life.

One of the most convincing cases was that of a six-year-old Indian boy named Ravi Shankar who insisted that he had been beheaded in his previous life by a jealous relative who had murdered him for his money. Although Ravi's parents were initially inclined to dismiss the story as a child's fantasy they thought it was far too morbid and specific to dismiss out of hand, so they casually probed him for more details and were given many that were later verified by the investigating authorities. But the most compelling evidence was the knife-shaped scar on their son's neck where the murderer's blade had severed his head from his body.

At the other end of the world, in Alaska, toddler Jimmy Svenson regaled his parents with stories of being his own uncle in a former life, who had

North American fisherman William George feared that one day he would drown, but in such an event he made a promise to try to return

died in suspicious circumstances. Again, the child's parents in this case were inclined to dismiss his statements as being the product of an over-active imagination. However, doctors had no explanation for the cluster of birthmarks on their son's abdomen – they resembled the scars that would form around bullet wounds. His uncle was believed to have been shot to death.

And then there was the remarkable case of Wijeratne, a Singhalese boy who had been born with a deformed arm. Wijeratne was just two when he first told his startled parents that his deformity was not a natural affliction but a punishment inflicted in a former life for having killed his wife. He even recalled his name in that former life, Ratran Hami. Wijeratne's parents did not make enquiries to test the validity of their son's story, but the boy was persistent. As he grew older his 'memory' returned and he was able to supply many more details of his former existence, including the circumstances which had led to the death of Ratran's wife, the weapon he had used and even the gist of his defence at the trial. All were subsequently verified by officials who were able to produce the transcripts of the trial and the official police reports.

But perhaps the most remarkable aspect of the case was that Wijeratne was finally able to settle the matter which had divided the community at the time of Ratran's conviction. His supporters had claimed that Ratran had accidentally stabbed his wife during a struggle while his detractors accused him of having murdered her in cold blood. The boy's 'confession' appeared to settle the matter.

But perhaps the most convincing case of all was that of North American fisherman William George, who told his son that he feared that one day he would drown but that if he did so he would make every effort to return as

his own grandson. Furthermore, he would have particular birthmarks to prove that he had kept his promise. Shortly afterwards, William's premonition came to pass. A year after his death, in May 1950, his daughter-in-law gave birth to a son who bore the birthmarks he had described. Moreover, as the boy grew up he affected certain mannerisms that were characteristic of his grandfather and he even identified the old man's watch although he had never seen it before.

IV

Children's Past Lives

Our birth is but a sleep and a forgetting;
The Soul that rises with us, our life's
Star, Hath had elsewhere its setting.
And cometh from afar.

William Wordsworth

WHEN YOUNG children speak of their past lives and of wanting to 'go home' to their 'real parents' their stories are frequently dismissed as the product of an active imagination. But when these longings persist, and sometimes even generate recurring nightmares, the parents have no option but to seek help from an experienced child counsellor. However, despite the weight of evidence, parents sometimes go into denial rather than accept the possibility that their son or daughter could be more than a mere child. In the following pages you will meet the boy, whose nightmares revealed a past life as a pilot trapped in a burning aircraft, the teenage girl who claimed to be the reincarnation of Anne Frank and the young son of Carol Bowman, whose experiences encouraged his mother to become a specialist in child regression therapy.

✣ SHANTI DEVI: ✣ I HAVE LIVED BEFORE

IN A SMALL VILLAGE near Delhi in the 1930s a young Indian girl stood patiently while a blindfold was tied around her head. But she was not playing a children's game. Shanti Devi was participating in a serious experiment upon which the validity of the entire nation's religious beliefs depended. India's most venerated figurehead, Mahatma Ghandi himself, had taken a personal interest in her case, going so far as to commission an independent study to ensure that her claims to be able to recall a previous life were to be tested under strict scientific conditions.

Shanti's story, which was to become one of the most thoroughly documented cases of reincarnation on record, began when she was just four years old. She had casually remarked to her parents that she missed her husband and children. When she was asked what she was talking about she told them that in her previous incarnation she had been a young mother called Ludgi who had lived in Muthra with her husband Kedarnath. She had died in 1925 while giving birth to their fourth child.

Being devout Hindus her parents took her claims seriously, but when she demanded to return to her 'real home' they feared their daughter might be delusional and so they took her to the local doctor. During her examination Shanti described medical procedures she should not have known about at such a tender age. But as there was nothing physically wrong with her she was allowed to return home where her parents made her promise to concentrate on the present.

'That was then, but this is now,' they told her. 'This time you are with us'.

But the past would not let Shanti be. She continued to talk of her previous life and in such detail that one of her teachers was prompted to write to the address the little girl had given as her 'real home' in Muthra, inquiring if a woman answering to the name of Ludgi had once lived there. Incredibly, Ludgi's husband wrote back confirming the essence of her story, including the existence of the other family members she had named and her claim to have died in childbirth. All she had said had been verified by the 'husband' she had never met, at least not in her present life.

More extraordinary still, an acquaintance of Shanti's father called unannounced shortly afterwards and the little girl immediately greeted him as her husband's cousin, although she had never seen him before. The astonished visitor confirmed that he lived in Muthra and that he did in fact have a cousin called Kedarnath whose wife had been named Ludgi. Shanti's parents then arranged for Kedarnath to visit and although he had never travelled to her village before she recognized him immediately.

Inevitably, the case aroused considerable interest in the press and it ultimately came to the attention of Ghandi and the government, who seized the chance to prove the central concept of Hindu belief for all the world to see. It was then that Shanti agreed to be blindfolded before leading a team of researchers through the streets of Muthra. There she identified landmarks from memory alone.

After the researchers had removed the blindfold, she was able to take them straight to Ludgi's house. There she was reunited with her children as well as her husband's parents and brother, all of whom she correctly identified. The only person she failed to recognize was the child that she had died giving birth to.

On a subsequent visit to the town, to see the house of Ludgi's mother, Shanti commented upon the changes that had been made to the property since her death and then she led the investigators to a place where Ludgi had hidden her jewellery. Not even her husband had known that the valuables were buried there.

Mahatma Ghandi took a personal interest in the case involving Shanti Devi, and sought to ensure that her claims were rigorously tested

✣ Return to Khriby ✣

THE CASE OF Shanti Devi is often cited as the most convincing case of its kind on record, but it is far from unique and, in fact, there are more remarkable cases which offer such a wealth of verifiable details that they almost defy one to deny them.

One such case is that of Imad Elawar, a young Lebanese boy whose claim to remember his former life was investigated by one of the most conscientious and tireless researchers into spontaneous past life recall – Dr Ian Stevenson, Professor of Psychiatry at the University of Virginia.

In 1964 Dr Stevenson travelled to the Lebanese village of Kornayel in order to meet five-year-old Imad and his family. Stevenson discovered that ever since he had learnt to speak the boy had been asking for a young woman called Jamile and a man called Mahmoud, but no members of his family answered to those names. He also expressed a wish to return to Khriby, a village which lay 30 kilometres over the mountains, which he

Dr Stevenson travelled to Kornayel to meet five-year-old Imad. His aim was to investigate the boy's remarkable claims of a past life

described in detail although he had never been outside his own village. He told his family that his previous surname had been Bouhamzy and he was said to have hugged a stranger in the street, whom he greeted as a former neighbour from his old home town. The man acknowledged that he had indeed lived in Khriby, but when Imad's father heard of this incident he was angry. Although his faith acknowledged the possibility of reincarnation, the father was uncomfortable with the idea that his son could be anything other than an innocent child.

More disturbing was the fact that the boy began to talk about a fatal accident in which a man's legs had been crushed under the wheels of a truck. The vivid picture he painted of the man's injuries and the description he gave of the unsuccessful operation he underwent at the hospital were upsetting enough for his father, but curiously the story seemed to involve the boy as well. Although Imad was adamant that he had not been the injured man in his previous life, he continually expressed his happiness that he was able to walk in his present life.

Stevenson questioned the boy at length and then journeyed over the mountain to Khriby to put his tale to the test. There he learned that there was indeed a local family by the name of Bouhamzy and that the father, Said, had died in the manner Imad had described. However, the house did not match Imad's description and neither did the other details of Said's life.

Undeterred, Dr Stevenson pursued his enquiries and soon discovered that Said had had a cousin called Ibrahim who had lived with Jamile, his beautiful mistress. Mahmoud had been the name of his uncle. In 1949, nine years before Imad was born, Ibrahim had died after a long illness in a house which Stevenson later saw for himself and agreed matched the boy's description. He was told that for the last months of his life Ibrahim had been confined to bed, where he brooded on the death of his cousin and his own inability to walk. As if that was not enough, Stevenson also obtained confirmation that the man Imad had embraced in the street had been the former neighbour of Ibrahim Bouhamzy.

That would have been enough to convince a typical researcher, but Stevenson was not satisfied. He returned to Kornayel where he persuaded Imad and his father to accompany him back to Khriby in the hope of unearthing more details of the boy's former life. On the journey to Khriby, one which Imad had never made before, the child described seven significant features of the landscape that were subsequently proved to be correct. When they reached their destination Imad offered fourteen further facts concerning Ibrahim's life which were confirmed. These included details of the furnishings of the house, which had been locked since its owner's death, and the exact location of the man's firearms.

Stevenson has not been without his critics, but his credibility as an investigator is above reproach. He investigated all of his cases personally, taking nothing on hearsay and always searched out several witnesses to corroborate everything he had been told. It is a sobering thought that men have been convicted on less evidence than Dr Stevenson has accumulated to make his case and yet many remain unconvinced.

The Hindu Who Dares to Disbelieve

CONTRARY TO POPULAR belief, not all Hindus believe in reincarnation. A minority consider it to be a harmful superstition which keeps the underprivileged 'in their place' and worse, is open to exploitation by the unscrupulous.

Television presenter Sanal Edamaruku is currently fronting a personal campaign against what he believes are bogus reincarnation claims. He says these are frequently put forward by poor parents in order to have one of their children adopted by a wealthier family and themselves compensated for their 'loss'. In a recent broadcast on India's national station, Star TV, he claims to have exposed a fraudulent case in which a father had tutored his three-year-old son to answer a series of questions in such a way that it would seem that he was the reincarnated spirit of a farmer who had died two years before the child was born.

The farmer had died from a gunshot wound to the throat and whenever an audience or a camera crew were present the child dutifully answered the same five questions as if he had learnt them by rote, even pointing to his neck when his father asked where he had been shot. But when Sanal reversed the order of the questions and asked the boy for his name, the child automatically pointed to his throat.

In another case, where a young Muslim woman had befriended a Hindu girl claiming that the younger child was the reincarnation of a beloved aunt, it was found that the older woman had invented the story to silence objections to her having a Hindu friend.

✣ DAVID SPANGLER ✣

A FOUNDER OF the Findhorn spiritual community and retreat in Scotland, David Spangler described his childhood glimpses into the last moments of a past life in his book *The Magic of Findhorn.*

> *I was having psychic experiences when I was a baby, before I could read. I can remember having experiences of a dual consciousness. I was observing a very large ship sinking; lifeboats were coming away from it. I had a strong sense of having to do something. I was aware of the fear and the panic. It was night time, and the lights of the ship were going out, boats were pulling away and the ship went down. I had this very strong impulse to seek help and remember clearly opening my eyes and seeing a crib, being completely disoriented, not knowing who or where I was, what I was doing in the crib or how old I was. I still thought that I was an adult, and tried to speak. I wanted to tell the people in the room who must have been my parents that the ship had sunk, but the only thing that came out was a squeal and a squeak, and within a few moments the adult sense was gone, and I remember nothing after that. I was very small. These experiences continued throughout my childhood.*

'I was observing a very large ship sinking... It was night time... and the ship went down'

When he was seven he had an experience which changed his outlook on life.

> *It was a sense of total identification with everything in the universe. David Spangler ceased to exist; an entirely different consciousness took over. In that moment I knew who I was. I had a sense of the eternality of my existence... There was no limit to my identity...*

The experience had a profound impact:

> *I didn't talk about it, but it completely altered my frame of reference. It was an experience of waking up.*

✣ FEAR OF FLYING ✣

AT SIX YEARS OLD James Leininger looked every inch a normal, happy child who might be seen running with a dog or fishing in a creek in his hometown of Lafayette, deep in the heart of Cajun country. But James was a troubled child, because from the age of two he had been haunted by recurrent nightmares from which his parents, Bruce and Andrea Leininger, had to shake him awake.

As often as four times a week his mother and father ran to his room to see him kicking, struggling and screaming, 'Airplane crash on fire, little man can't get out'.

Nothing that James had seen, heard or read could explain the trauma he was evidently experiencing. Both parents had been careful to shield him from violent TV programmes and neither of them could recall any incident or discussion which might account for their son's irrational fear. It wasn't flying that he was afraid of – it was the fear of being trapped in a burning plane, a fear that was inexplicable in a young child.

Time and again, while playing with his toy planes he would crash them into the dining table which served as the carrier base and yell, 'Plane crash – on fire!'

It was only when Andrea's mother suggested that the trauma might originate in her grandson's past life that things started to improve. On her mother's recommendation, Andrea contacted counsellor Carol Bowman, author of *Children's Past Lives: How Past Life Memories Affect Your Child*. She was advised to talk to James about the nightmares in a calm, matter-of-fact manner, in order to draw out any details that she might be able to verify. Instead of treating the nightmares as symptoms of an over-active imagination or neurosis, she discussed them as if they were deep-seated memories that needed to be teased out and dealt with.

'When we are dreaming, our conscious minds are not filtering material as when we are in a waking state, so unconscious material, including past

> *'James suffered from recurrent nightmares, and kept screaming, "Airplane crash on fire, little man can't get out."'*

US Navy Corsairs on the deck of an aircraft carrier: James Leininger related how he had flown a Corsair along with details of events leading up to his 'death'

life memories, emerges,' Bowman explained. 'On some level, they are seeking resolution to these disturbing memories.'

As a result of his talks with his parents, the boy's fears were exorcized and the nightmares decreased, but the 'memories' did not fade away. In fact, they intensified. He began recalling specific details about his aircraft, the carrier that had served as his base and the events leading up to his 'death'. He gave them the name of his wingman in the squadron, Jack Larsen, and the name of the carrier, the *Natoma*. He also told them that his name had also been James then and that he had flown a Corsair. He even pointed out the precise location of the crash site in an aerial photograph. It was in the Pacific, off the island of Chichi Jima near Iwo Jima.

Determined to get to the bottom of this 'fantasy', which he still believed it to be, his father searched the Internet, armed with the details he had been given. He was stunned to discover that a carrier by the name of the USS *Natoma Bay* had been stationed in the Pacific during the invasion of Iwo Jima. Redoubling his efforts, he then went in search of Jack Larsen, taking the trouble to travel to a veteran's reunion to talk to Larsen face to face, but without revealing the nature of his enquiry. Larsen confirmed that he had served in the squadron based on the *Natoma* and that he had been the wingman for a pilot named James M. Huston jun., who had been reported missing in action during a raid over Futami Ko Harbor at Chichi Jima in 1945. Huston was just twenty-one years old and he would have been on his way home after the mission had he not been shot down that day.

At around this time, James was given three GI Joe dolls. He called them Walter, Leon and Billie and his father was to learn that these were the

names of three pilots who had served with Huston and who had been killed in action.

Asked why he had given the dolls those names the boy remarked, 'Because they greeted me when I went to heaven'.

Even then, Bruce Leininger was not seriously considering the possibility that his son was the reincarnation of James Huston jun., but that somehow the spirit of the young pilot was speaking through the boy. Incredibly, he

There was one discrepancy in the boy's story: James Huston's plane was officially listed as an FM2 Wildcat fighter, not a Corsair

still held out hope that it was all a child's fantasy and that the verified facts were no more than a string of uncanny coincidences. It all hinged on one small but significant discrepancy – Huston's plane was listed in the official records as an FM2 Wildcat fighter and not a Corsair as the boy maintained. All of the veterans Bruce had contacted had confirmed that Corsairs had not been assigned to the *Natoma*.

Even so, Bruce was not content to leave a crumb of doubt.

In spring 2003 he managed to trace Huston's 86-year-old sister, Anne, who was then living in California, from whom he obtained several photos of her brother taken during the war. One of these set Bruce back on his heels. It showed the young pilot standing proudly in front of a Corsair – the plane he had flown the year before his death when he was in an elite squadron known as the Devil's Disciples (Squadron VF-301).

'Lightning can strike once, but when it strikes eight or nine times, you can't say it's a coincidence,' Bruce confessed to a local reporter when the story became news.

When James Huston's mother heard the full story in October 2003 she took a while assimilate the full implications, but then she sent a letter of support to the Leininger family, together with some of her son's treasured personal effects.

'This child couldn't know the things he does,' her daughter told reporter Wes Milligan of *Acadiana Profile* magazine, 'he just couldn't – so I believe he is somehow a part of my brother.'

Carol Bowman, who subsequently investigated the case following the initial contact from the boy's mother, believes that:

> *If a soul reincarnates with 'unfinished business', or dies a traumatic death, these memories are more likely to carry over into another life… As I see it, a part of James Huston's consciousness survived death and is a part of James Leininger's soul consciousness. The present incarnation is not a carbon copy of the last, but contains aspects of James Huston's personality and experience.*

Postscript

THE CASE OF James Leininger has a counterpart in that of an unnamed boy in Mary Harrison's book *Life Before Birth*. On his fifth birthday the boy drew the cockpit of a plane. He told his astonished parents that he had flown the plane and died in it. He correctly positioned every dial, gauge and lever and explained the function of each one of them, including the button that released the bombs. Further questioning revealed details of the facilities at the airbase which included the little-known fact that the washbasins did not have taps, but a pump. This was clearly not a little boy's heroic fantasy because several years earlier he had drawn the insignia that had appeared on his uniform and that of his comrades. It was a swastika.

✦ An Interview with ✦ Carol Bowman

CAROL BOWMAN, MS., is widely regarded as one of America's foremost past life regression therapists and is a pioneer in reincarnation studies. Her bestselling book, *Children's Past Lives* (Bantam, 1997), was the first non-academic study into the phenomenon of children's spontaneous past life memories. Since its publication Carol has appeared on *Oprah, Good Morning America* and the *Discovery Channel*, where she has offered advice to parents who suspect that their children's fears and phobias might originate in a previous life.

The following interview with Carol Bowman was conducted by the author.

Q: ***Your work with children and their past lives began with helping your own son and daughter to process their recollections of a previous incarnation. Could you describe how those experiences helped them and developed into your present practice?***

Carol: My interest in children's past lives began when my five-year-old son, Chase, developed a hysterical fear of loud booming sounds. This phobia seemed to appear suddenly one night when he heard a fireworks show; the loud booming sounds terrified him. A few weeks later, it happened again: when Chase was around loud booming sounds he became hysterical. I couldn't understand where his fear had come from.

When a skilled hypnotherapist friend was visiting, we simply asked Chase to close his eyes and tell us what he saw when he was afraid of these loud sounds. Immediately Chase recounted a detailed story of being an adult soldier on a battlefield.

'I'm standing behind a rock,' he began. 'I'm carrying a long gun with a kind of sword at the end.'

'What are you wearing?' the therapist asked.

'I have dirty, ripped clothes, brown boots, a belt. I'm hiding behind a rock, crouching on my knees and shooting at the enemy. I'm at the edge of a valley. The battle is going on all around me.'

I was amazed to hear this, particularly as Chase had never been interested in war toys, and had never even owned a toy gun. He always preferred building things with Lego and playing with his wooden trains. We restricted his television viewing to pre-school programmes such as *Sesame Street* and up to that time he hadn't seen a war movie.

'I'm behind a rock,' he continued. 'I don't want to look, but I have to when I shoot. Smoke and flashes everywhere. And loud noises: yelling,

Carol's five-year-old son Chase was terrified of loud noises and experienced vivid recurring images of being a soldier in battle

screaming, loud booms. I'm not sure who I'm shooting at – there's so much smoke, so much going on. I'm scared. I shoot at anything that moves. I really don't want to be here and shoot other people.'

The other striking aspect was that Chase's tone was serious and mature – uncharacteristic of my carefree five-year-old. He really seemed to be reliving this soldier's emotions and recalling his impressions of the scene he was witnessing. If it had been a fantasy, surely it would have been exciting and he would have pictured himself in a heroic role. In contrast, these were the thoughts of a frightened and confused young man who was horrified of the idea of killing another human being and afraid for his own survival. He was sitting on my lap at the time and I could sense his body tensing up. His breath quickened and he curled himself into a ball which indicated that he was uncomfortable with facing this experience again, to say the least.

This was clearly not a child's fantasy. He described how he was shot in the wrist, how he missed his wife and family (!), and his ambivalence about being a soldier. My friend the therapist talked calmly and in a common sense manner to put Chase at his ease. He explained that soldiers are trained to kill other men in order to survive themselves and that there is no blame or guilt attached to doing one's duty so long as the enemy were also armed.

'We live many different lives on earth,' he told him. 'We take turns playing different parts, like actors in a play. We learn what it means to be human by playing these different parts. Sometimes we are soldiers and kill others in a battle, and sometimes we are killed. We are simply playing our parts to learn.'

As he listened to these assurances, I could feel my son's body relax and his breathing become more regular. The anguished look on his face melted away. After this brief recollection, not only did his fear of loud booming sounds completely disappear, but a chronic eczema on his wrist, on the very spot where he said he had been shot in the other life, also disappeared. He had had the eczema since he was a baby, and it had not responded to any medical treatments we tried. We had tried everything. But within a few days of his recollection, the eczema went away completely, never to return.

In my daughter's case, she had always been terrified of our house burning. We had not really become aware of it until she became hysterical when she saw a movie with an explosion and a fire scene in it. We did the same thing with her: we told her to tell us what she saw in her mind when she thought about fires. She emotionally recounted the death of a young girl in a house fire. After that brief recollection, her phobia went away, just as her brother's had.

These two experiences, which happened on the same afternoon, got me hooked. I started talking to other parents to see if they had experienced anything like that with their own children, and I read whatever I could find on past lives, trying to understand how these phobias originated, and why they disappeared so suddenly after the children recalled these apparent previous lives. I was most intrigued by Chase's physical healing after his recollection. I saw that these memories might have vast implications for children – and adults. These memories were so easy to access in my children, and the results were so profound. It seemed that others should have had similar experiences.

'I could feel my son's body relax and his breathing become more regular. The anguished look on his face melted away'

Q: ***How did your training as a counsellor contribute to uncovering children's past lives and have you found that counselling techniques such as mirroring and paraphrasing are more reliable in the type of regression you practise than hypnosis? And do you agree that hypnosis risks leading the subject or encourages them to produce details to please the therapist?***

Carol: After doing this research for about five years, I decided that I wanted to train as a counsellor to legitimize my findings and learn the rudiments of counselling to enhance my skills. So I went to graduate school and got a degree in counselling.

My past life regression practice is with teens and adults. I do not regress young children. Rather, I counsel parents whose very young children (under the age of seven) are having *spontaneous* past life recollections. I offer them guidance in my two books, too.

When I work with adults, I help them access their past lives through their present feelings, thoughts, and physical sensations. It's really about focusing on their present feelings and deepening them. Past life regression is an art: walking a fine line between guiding and leading the client. The less leading, the better, in my opinion. But some leading is necessary to guide a client through a memory, so they feel safe enough to access difficult memories, if they should come up. Also, I've found that it's difficult for people to get the full past life story on their own; they get stuck at some point and can't move through it. It's just the nature of the experience. Having said that, some individuals have spontaneous recollections and get the full experience that way – the story, the meaning, and its implications to their present lives.

Comparing children's spontaneous memories and past life regression with adults, is like comparing apples to oranges. They're both ways of accessing past life memories, but they are really two distinct processes. With young children, the memories are very close to the surface, until around the age of seven, and emerge spontaneously, or are manifested in their present personality. With adults, who have had years of experience and conditioning, it requires deepening techniques, such as relaxation and hypnosis, to access the memories. They are not as readily available as with young children.

Q: ***Why do some children recall their previous lives and not others? Is it only those who have unfinished business or trauma to deal with, or can it be down to the responsiveness of the parents?***

Carol: I believe that many children express past life memories, but most adults in the West are not aware of what is happening. Especially if a child talks about a benign or positive lifetime, it is more likely to be dismissed as fantasy. It seems that the memories that are most noticeable in children are those relating to traumatic deaths, or lingering feelings from a previous life. Many children talk about their previous deaths, which gets the adults' attention.

Most of these deaths are traumatic. These deaths imprint in a similar way as post-traumatic stress disorder that we see in present-life situations. The difference is that the trauma is not from this life, but another. But it can act in the same way: the child can be stuck in the shock, sadness, or fear from the previous death. If they're allowed to talk about it, they can move through it.

Q: ***Have you had any problems with hardened sceptics or religious fundamentalists who feel threatened by having their beliefs questioned by the concept of reincarnation? Has anyone tried to fool you by faking a case and what would be your criteria for testing the validity of their story?***

Carol: I'm really not concerned with religious fundamentalists or hardened sceptics. No matter what kind of evidence is presented to them, they've already made up their minds that reincarnation is impossible. So why waste any energy on that?

I'm not aware of any fraudulent cases that have been presented to me. If I find a case that lacks substance, I don't spend any time with it.

Carol's daughter's fear diminished after she recalled dying as a child in a house fire

Q: ***Does your experience suggest that all phobias originate in a past life and can you please give an example where a phobia has been cured by regression.***

Carol: Certainly many phobias in children can relate to present-life experiences. Unfortunately, many young children are exposed to abuse, they witness war or violence, they lose a parent or sibling, they suffer an illness. The list is long. But some phobias which cannot be traced to anything the child has experienced can relate to a past life.

In my own two children's cases, Chase's phobia of loud sounds disappeared after he recalled dying on a battlefield behind a cannon; in my daughter's case, her fear of fire greatly diminished after she recalled dying as a child in a house fire. I've had many other cases in which phobias that directly related to the past-life deaths diminished or disappeared after they talked about their previous lives.

Q: *Are you finding that parents are now becoming more willing to have their children undertake counselling and to take the possibility of a past life origin for problems more seriously? Is there a danger, however, that some parents and the less experienced counsellors might assume the origin of a problem is in the child's past life and not look any further? Or is this not a problem so long as the issue is resolved? Is this what you mean when you say that you are not so interested in proving that the 'memory' is genuine, only in ensuring there is healing, growth and understanding for that child?*

Carol: I think there is a danger in attributing a child's phobia or anxiety or anger to a past life without thoroughly investigating origins in the present life. Any responsible therapist wouldn't jump to a past life explanation first. However, I've worked with teens who have been in counselling, and after hitting a wall in therapy, they find that their problems really did originate in another life. Sometimes the issues can resolve fairly quickly if the past life story is uncovered.

Unfortunately, there are precious few therapists in the United States and in Europe who are trained to work with children and are trained in past life therapy. So it's really not that easy to find a therapist who will work on the past life level with a child.

Q: *You list four things that a parent can use to distinguish fact from fantasy. What other criteria do you use during a course of 'treatment'.*

Carol: When I counsel parents about their young children, I get a full history of that child – from conception forward. I am looking for any statements, behaviours, unusual situations, physical symptoms – any clues I can get – that might shed some light on the child. I am listening as a counsellor and a detective. Sometimes, when a parent starts giving the history of the child, little details start popping into place and present a fuller picture of the child, and a possible past life story.

Q: *Can you describe a typical session and course of sessions (i.e., how you tease out these memories and what other techniques you might use to help the child integrate these thoughts, emotions and images). Do you encourage them to draw, write stories, etc.?*

Carol: There is no typical session, since I don't work directly with the young children, but encourage the parents to respond appropriately to the child.

During play, children may talk to past life characters or re-enact unfinished business from a previous existence

Children may re-enact their past lives through their repetitive play activities. They might talk to past life characters as they play, or re-enact some unfinished business from the past. Drawing, storytelling, sand play and other activities may be good outlets for these memories to emerge.

Q: ***So many cultures have been built on the belief in an afterlife and of the transmigration of souls – why do you think it is that***

so many people today still stubbornly deny the possibility of the existence of the soul and of reincarnation? What is it in the human psyche that denies the evidence of its own eyes – the cycle of the seasons, the regeneration in nature.

Carol: People have been persecuted for centuries for a belief in reincarnation. Brainwashing has been most effective in convincing people that they're not seeing what is before them. If people are interested in this aspect they will find more in a chapter of my book titled *Adults and Their Religions*.

Q: ***Do you find that the medical profession now takes regression and reincarnation more seriously?***

'The medical profession may never accept reincarnation and past lives as the cause for present personality traits'

Carol: I think that the medical profession may never accept reincarnation and past lives as the cause for present personality traits and even physical symptoms. But isolated professionals are coming to this conclusion on their own. It's a very slow process.

Q: ***Many people consult psychics rather than a professional counsellor or regression therapist and claim to have received guidance and information on their past lives that has proven helpful. How do you view this particular avenue of exploration?***

Carol: There are genuine psychics who can tune in to a person's past lives. This information can be helpful to some. However, it is my feeling that accessing one's own past life story - and reliving or re-experiencing the emotions of it – has a much more profound healing effect. The meaning of the past life and its implications in the present becomes more apparent when one experiences it oneself.

Q: ***Finally, if there was one case or incident of which you have personal experience that sums up the benefits of regression or past life counselling which one would that be?***

Carol: In my own case, one past life regression reversed the course of a chronic illness (included in the first book and on my website). In two lifetimes that I saw, I died first of consumption, then in a gas chamber in the Second World War. After the session, my chronic lung problems improved dramatically. That's why I wanted to learn to become a past life therapist.

Steve's Story

CAROL CUT the following case study from *Children's Past Lives* but gave permission for it to be published here for the first time because it illustrates how past-life recollections can emerge in our dreams before they manifest as physical symptoms and neurosis if not treated in time.

Steve's memories of dying in the Holocaust began as childhood nightmares. Throughout his life, these dreams and memories lurked just below the surface of consciousness, affecting him in many ways: as phobias, physical ailments, and an innate talent. When Steve was born in 1955, he was unable to digest food and spent the first year of his life in the hospital; he was officially 'allergic to everything'. He also had frequent childhood nightmares about trying to climb the walls of his bedroom. In these dreams he was always a woman and, upon wakening, would find himself repeating a seemingly meaningless word that sounded like 'vendorswagens'. In school he wrote accounts of escaping from camp and being wrongly accused, stories which caused serious concern among his teachers.

At the age of sixteen, Steve 'miraculously' started playing quality piano without having been trained! But there was a dark side to this musical talent. Every time Steve sat down at the piano, he had nightmarish visions of playing for many thin, starving children. He would try to make the children laugh but could only cry inside because he knew they were dying. These impressions were so overwhelming that sometimes Steve could not go on playing. But it was a mysterious phobia which finally drove Steve to consult a hypnotherapist. For some unknown reason, Steve's neck was always extremely sensitive, and he could not stand to have anyone touch it. The very thought was terrifying. He knew this fear was not logical, but it would not go away. Eventually, with the help of the hypnotherapist, the following story unfolded.

In another life Steve had been a young Belgian woman who journeyed to Paris and got a job playing piano in a Jewish-owned nightclub. Through a series of mishaps, she was deported to Poland and falsely accused of being a Jew. This woman was not sent to a concentration camp at first, but to 'a part of town where we were all crowded together – starving, dirty'. Every morning Poles would come with carts to carry away the dead – carts that were called 'vendorswagens', the strange word from Steve's childhood dreams. While in this ghetto, the woman entertained the starving children

As a child, Steve wrote stories about escaping from a concentration camp, an event which he later found out belonged to a past life

with her piano playing, trying to take away some of the sting of the deplorable conditions in which they were forced to live. But eventually, this woman was deported to a concentration camp. She and a friend attempted to escape, were recaptured, and then hung. At the moment of death, this woman felt ashamed to face anyone, as if she had somehow let them down by failing to escape and get help. This feeling, along with the choking sensation of hanging, apparently carried over into the next life, which accounted for Steve's sensitive neck.

Steve's story is particularly interesting, because he had all three signs of past life dreams: his dreams were vivid and coherent, they were recurring and he saw himself in a distinctly different persona – as a grown woman. Knowledge beyond experience was evident in his touch of xenoglossy: the word 'vendorswagen', which represented the essence of all the horror he had witnessed during the death watch in the ghastly ghetto – so much so that it stuck with him into this life. Steve had physical traits relating to his hanging in the past, and a natural ability to play the piano, just as he had done in his former life. As a child, he even wrote stories about escaping from camp and being falsely accused – which, he later found out, was exactly what had happened to him in his past life. But no one recognized these signs of Steve's past life memory. It wasn't until Steve was an adult that he sought the help of a hypnotherapist to understand the sensitivity in his neck. With the hypnotherapist's help, his full past life story was revealed. The shame and guilt that shrouded his past life death was finally shed.

A fuller account of this case can be found in Rabbi Gershom's book *Beyond The Ashes*.

✣ The Return of Anne Frank? ✣

ONE OF THE most moving stories of the Second World War is that of Anne Frank, the young Jewish girl whose diary records her experiences while hiding out in an attic with her family during the Nazi occupation of Holland. The family were ultimately betrayed and deported to Belsen concentration camp where they were murdered in 1945, but Anne's diary – which became a perennial bestseller and is now required reading for schoolchildren around the world – remains a testimony to human courage. However, no one could have imagined that there might have been a sequel of some sort.

In 1954 a two-year-old Swedish girl, Barbro Karlen, told her bemused parents that she did not want to call them 'ma' and 'pa' because they were not her real parents and besides, her name was not Barbro but Anne Frank. At that time no one knew of Anne Frank for her diary had not yet been published.

As she grew up Barbro insisted that her 'real' parents would one day come to take her home, but more disquieting was the frustration that her mother and father felt in being unable to comfort her whenever she suffered from a series of recurring nightmares. These always began with Barbro cowering in the dark, fearing for her life as the sound of heavy boots approached on the stairs outside the attic in which she was hiding. The next moment the door would be kicked in and she would wake in a cold sweat, screaming for her parents.

But these were not the only symptoms of what her parents thought must be an uncommonly vivid fantasy. Barbro had an irrational fear of men in uniform, a strong aversion to beans (which had been the Frank family's only source of food for two long years) and she would only take a bath, refusing ever to take a shower. The victims of Belsen had been gassed in the shower block at the camp.

To appease her worried parents she made no mention of her 'memories' during an interview with a child psychiatrist and so was considered a 'normal' child. But as she approached her teens she became confused when the subject of Anne Frank was discussed at school. In her naïveté she wondered how her teachers could know about this little girl whose memories and fears she had shared. More significantly, she wondered how it was possible for her to be two people at the same time.

The answers came when, at the age of ten, she accompanied her parents on a tour of Europe. During a stopover in Amsterdam her parents planned to visit the Anne Frank House which had been turned into a museum. But before her father could call a taxi Barbro had persuaded them that they could walk there. Although their daughter had never set foot outside Sweden she led her mother and father through the twisting streets of Amsterdam for a full ten minutes until they came to the door of the Achterhuis on the Prinsengracht. While her parents stood speechless, Barbro expressed disappointment at the changes that had been made to the façade. Then, as they ascended the narrow staircase, hand in hand, Barbro's mother noticed that her daughter's face was drained of colour, her hand had grown clammy and cold and she was breathing with difficulty.

When they entered one of the upstairs rooms Barbro brightened and exclaimed excitedly, 'Look, the pictures of the film stars are still there!'

But when her parents looked they could see nothing but bare walls. Intrigued, they asked one of the tour guides if there had at one time been pictures and magazine cuttings on the wall and they were told that they had recently been taken down so that they could be mounted under glass to preserve them.

When Barbro Karlen visited Anne Frank's house, she saw things others couldn't and had to run from the building

Her parents were keen to question their daughter further, but Barbro couldn't remain a moment longer. Her initial joy at 'coming home' was being smothered by a feeling of wretchedness and a profound sense of loss. She ran from the building in tears and collapsed in the street.

The visit had a profound effect on her mother who began to take an interest in spiritual matters, but her father could not accept the possibility of reincarnation as it conflicted with his Christian upbringing.

'I can't deny that you have somehow been here before,' he told her. 'Perhaps you have lived before and reincarnated, but you are the only one!'

Her mother's support was a great comfort, but it was only when Barbro began to record her thoughts in a journal in the form of short essays and poems that she felt she could make sense of her experiences. Her writing impressed a family friend who suggested that she should submit it to a publisher. The book, *Man on Earth*, was an instant bestseller and at the tender age of twelve Barbro became a minor celebrity, debating the implication of reincarnation with priests and theologians on national television.

During her teenage years Barbro wrote a further eight books, before she finally wrote directly of her past life memories when in her forties, raising the possibility that – assuming she was the reincarnation of Anne Frank – she had been given a second chance to fulfil Anne's stated ambition to become a great writer.

✣ From the Ashes ✣

THERE ARE THOSE who strongly object to the suggestion that the victims of the Nazis might have been reborn in order to find the fulfilment they were denied in their previous lives. They feel that it diminishes the horror of the Holocaust. If every wrong can be made right, it would mean that those who committed the atrocities would be absolved from the responsibility of their actions. Such 'happy endings', the critics would say, are the wish fulfilment fantasies of those who cannot face reality, and worse, they risk diminishing the crimes of racial persecution and even murder.

There are those who survived the extermination of their families in the Nazi death camps and who remain haunted by what they have seen. They continue to suffer the loss of their loved ones every single day of their lives. Telling those among the bereaved who believe in reincarnation that their loved ones might have been reborn does not bring them closure or diminish the pain – it only gives them hope. Giving the same message to those who do not believe in reincarnation only intensifies the anguish because it is demeaning to the memory of those they have lost.

But the subject needs to be examined because if such cases as that of Barbro are genuine it would prove that the human spirit cannot be extinguished, that evil acts are self-defeating and must ultimately fail. Once this idea is understood there can be no more Holocausts.

In spite of everything, I still really believe
that people are really good at heart.

Anne Frank

UNANSWERED QUESTIONS

As the author of two books about reincarnation and the Holocaust, Rabbi Gershom was initially sceptical about Barbro's claims

IN HIS REVIEW of Barbro's fictionalized autobiography *And The Wolves Howled* (Perseus Verlag, Basel, 1997) for *Life and Soul* magazine (1999), Rabbi Yonassan Gershom, himself the author of two books on reincarnation and the Holocaust – *Beyond the Ashes: Cases of Reincarnation from the Holocaust* (A.R.E. Press, Virginia Beach VA, 1992) and *From Ashes To Healing* – admitted that he was initially sceptical of Karlen's claims.

> *I had already been contacted by four other people who also claimed to be Anne Frank, along with a plethora of Hitlers, Mengeles, and other characters from the Second World War. Although I have written two books about cases of reincarnation from the Holocaust, I am cautious about individuals who claim to be the return of famous people. Because the biographies of historical figures are so well-known, it is very difficult to sort fact from fiction.*

As Rabbi Gershom pointed out, the case of Anne Frank was public knowledge through the publication of the book, the attendant publicity, documentaries and even a Hollywood dramatization. Her name had become synonymous with injustice and the Holocaust, raising the possibility that Barbro's 'memories' may simply have been the result of her subconsciously identifying with Anne Frank as the archetypal innocent victim.

Josef Mengele, Auschwitz's 'Angel of Death': many people claim to have lived previous lives as well-known characters from World War Two

As for Barbro's claim that she 'saw' the magazine clippings on the bare wall of the Frank house, Gershom offers an equally plausible explanation that does not involve reincarnation.

> *... one could also argue that what [Barbro] saw on the wall was not a scene from her own past life, but, rather, a psychic impression left on the 'aether' of the house itself.*

> *Anne Frank spent over two years living in the secret apartment and, as she tells us in her diary, much of that time was passed in motionless silence. She literally spent hours alone in her room, writing in her diary and dreaming of her beloved movie stars, in order to relieve the boredom. Is it possible that the mind-energy that she invested in that wall of photos has left a lasting impression, which [Barbro] 'saw' when she entered the room?*

Gershom concedes that Barbro might well be the reincarnation of someone who perished in the Holocaust, but not necessarily Anne Frank. Her situation and experiences were, tragically, typical, not unique.

> *In addition, there are some things in the book which strike me more as a psychological identification with the imagery of the Holocaust. For example, much of the story centers on how Sara [Barbro] was harassed and maligned in this life, first by her schoolmates because she was a child prodigy, and later by her colleagues on the police force, because she was among the first mounted policewomen in Sweden. In the end, what began as sexist hazing soon developed into a full-blown vendetta, with ugly rumors, false accusations, sabotage, vicious attacks in the press, and attempts on her life. The very title of the book,* And the Wolves Howled, *is a reference to this senseless hate campaign.*

'One could argue that what Barbro saw was a psychic impression left on the "aether' of the house itself'

One apparent inconsistency which does not bother Gershom is Barbro's lack of Jewish identity, but then the Frank family were not Orthodox and did not even commemorate Yom Kippur, the most solemn day in the Jewish calendar. In contrast, Anne records the great pleasure with which the family celebrated Christmas in their attic hide-out.

Gershom concludes his review of the book and the case by saying:

> *For my part, I do not doubt Karlen's sincerity. I am even willing to believe she was killed by the Nazis in another life. But was she really Anne Frank? The jury is still out.*

When Rabbi Gershom is asked if his own work, *Beyond the Ashes: Cases of Reincarnation from the Holocaust*, minimizes the responsibility of the Nazis for their crimes, he answers:

> *Exactly the opposite! My work holds the Nazis responsible not only for the death of the body, but also for the anguish of the soul. The Nazis did not seek to kill the body only – they also sought to destroy the Jewish identity and spirit forever. Many of those Jewish souls who came back as Gentiles did so because they were so horribly treated by the Nazis, that they could no longer bear the shame and pain that was put on them for*

Public humiliation: supervised by Nazis, elderly Jews are compelled to scrub the pavements of Vienna in 1938

being Jews. They came back as Gentiles because they wanted to be loved and to be safe from persecution.

So these stories do NOT minimize the Holocaust. They demonstrate how very deeply the Jewish people were wounded by the tortures in the camps, and how this pain carried down from one incarnation to the next, and how it will take many lifetimes to set it right again. Such a deep, deep tragedy! It adds yet another layer to the enormity of the Holocaust, because it means that this was not just a historical event in one century only, but also an event that is engraved on the souls of the Jewish people for many incarnations to come. So from these stories,

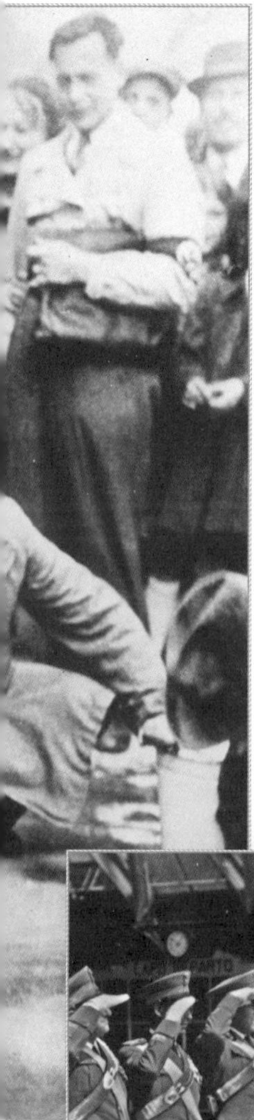

we can all learn something about how destructive prejudice and abuse are on the human soul and psyche.

In his second book on the subject, *From Ashes To Healing*, Rabbi Gershom writes:

> *Why did the Holocaust happen? There is no single answer, no pat reply that will put it to rest forever. Was it a karmic payback, a divine punishment, a learning experience, a fulfillment of prophecy, a mass martyrdom, or the birth pangs of the Messianic Age? Could all of these explanations have some measure of truth in different cases?*
>
> *Perhaps the answer lies within the very process of asking the question. Like a Zen koan, 'Why the Holocaust?' forces us to examine our hearts over and over, from all possible angles. Each time we ask the question again, we break through another layer of old thought patterns to confront the world in new ways.*

Why did the Holocaust happen? The question forces us to examine our hearts over and over, from all possible angles

V

The Case for Reincarnation

As long as you are not aware of the
continual law of Die and Be Again,
you are merely a vague guest
on a dark Earth.

Johann Wolfgang von Goethe

IT IS IRONIC that many psychiatrists (whose title translates as 'healers of the soul') do not believe in the human spirit on principle because its existence cannot be proven to their satisfaction. They ask why they should believe in reincarnation when there is no scientific evidence that proves the existence of the soul. But there is compelling empirical evidence from very credible sources. The following cases are just the tip of a substantial body of research. What marks them out from typical cases of recovered memories is the credibility of the witnesses and the considerable thoroughness of the research they undertook before they would even consider that their experiences might be genuine. One also raises the radical new theory that we might bring back more than memories from a previous life – we might actually look like our former selves!

• THE FACE IN THE MIRROR •

TO BE TOLD THAT you have lived before is not an easy thing to accept. It is even more difficult to believe that the images you have seen during regression are genuine memories of a past life and can be a truly life-transforming experience. But to actually relive the events of your past life when that life ended violently can be a shattering experience. That was what happened to retired Connecticut fire chief Jeffrey Keane, who unexpectedly found himself back in time at the battle of Antietam, a significant engagement in the American Civil War.

Jeffrey had never expressed an interest in the Civil War and hadn't even read a book on the subject when he and his wife, Anna, stopped off in Sharpsburg, Maryland during a summer vacation in May 1991. Jeffrey shared Anna's love for antiques, but even his interest was beginning to wane after they had visited every store in town.

General George B. McClellan at the Battle of Antietam – Jeffrey Keane took an audio tape tour of the site, which led him suddenly back into the past

Taking a break, the couple drove outside the town to the battlefield where Anna remained in the car while her husband explored the site. He decided to take an audio tape tour which described the events of that bloody September in 1862 when the Confederate army of General Robert E. Lee engaged the Union troops under General George B. McClellan in one of the bloodiest battles of the conflict.

When the tape finished Jeffrey did not join the other casual sightseers as they made their way back to their coaches and cars because something was nagging at him, something was compelling him to return and explore a dirt track, known as Sunken Road, where a rebel colonel and his men had held the enemy at bay at great cost. There, to his horror, he was suddenly overcome by a wave of grief, sadness and anger. Tears coursed down his face and he began to have difficulty breathing. It needs to be remembered that this is a man who had risked his life many times to rescue people from burning buildings and was inured to the sight of charred bodies. He had been trained to remain calm under extreme stress and make life-saving decisions in extremely hazardous situations.

At Sunken Road, to his horror Keane was suddenly overcome by a wave of grief, sadness and anger. Tears coursed down his face

Of course, this episode could have been merely the welling up of long-repressed emotions from his days as a firefighter, or even a reaction to the residual emotions of those who had died in the battle, but Jeffrey was a clear-headed, pragmatic man in control of his feelings and not given to outbursts of emotion. He was left drained and exhausted, so much so that he had difficulty walking back to the car. By the time he got back he had recovered his composure. He said nothing to Anna, partly because he had no idea what had occurred.

He thought nothing more about it until eighteen months later.

In October 1992 the couple were invited to a Halloween party at which the guests could have psychic readings given by an experienced local medium. Jeff thought this might be an opportunity to find out if his experience at Antietam was significant or not. Without prompting, the medium described the battle and in particular the skirmish at Sunken Road. She told Jeff that she 'saw' him there in his former life as a Confederate colonel and informed him that he had been seriously wounded at the very spot where he had been overcome by emotion 130 years later. More extraordinary still, she described him leaving his apparently lifeless body and hovering over the scene screaming 'No!' as his men were about to return fire.

'That's not right,' Jeff corrected her. 'I didn't say "no", I yelled "Not yet".'

Keane appeared to have inherited faint traces of the scars that Colonel Gordon (above) was left with after his wounds had healed

Jeff didn't know where that knowledge came from or why such an apparently insignificant detail could be so important, but the next day he pulled out *Civil War Quarterly*, a magazine he had bought at Sharpsburg as a souvenir, but hadn't looked at since. In fact he hadn't even flicked through it at the time. But now he opened it at a page featuring a photograph of Sunken Road and there a caption caught his eye.

'Not yet!' It was the last order Colonel Gordon had given his men as the Union troops had rushed towards them.

He had wanted them to hold their fire until the enemy were just a hundred yards away and when they had done so the withering volley was lethal. But the next instant Gordon himself was hit by musket balls. He was struck twice in the right leg, once in the right shoulder and again in the left arm. Then he suffered a bullet in the face and lost consciousness. When his body was carried from the field he was not expected to live. But miraculously he survived and went on to record the details of the battle in a journal that was to prove an invaluable source of information when Jeff later came to verify the details he had gleaned from other sources.

On looking at the photo in the magazine Jeff felt the same tide of emotion welling up within him that he had felt before, but then he saw the photo of Colonel Gordon on the opposite page and time stood still once more.

'This time a chill ran through me,' he remembers, 'and the hair on the back of my neck stood up again… The face was not unknown to me, I know it well, I shave it every morning.'

But that was not all. Jeff appeared to have inherited faint traces of the scars Gordon had suffered after his wounds had healed. He stared at the photo.

> *… something caught my eye, a line that started at mid-ear and zigzagged across his cheek, almost like a lightning streak… On the right side of my face starting at mid-ear is a scar, light but discernible. It moves across my cheek in a zigzag pattern. Under my left eye there is an area about the size of a quarter, indented a little with a jagged line outlining most of it. I*

MR. CHARLES DICKENS'S LAST READING.

looked at the photo [of Colonel Gordon] again and did a second double take. The mark on the left side of my face was in the same place as the entry wound under Gordon's eye. I was not only receiving confirmation of a past life, I was being beaten over the head with it.

Based on his standard method of comparison, Dr Semkiw claims J.K. Rowling is the reincarnation of Charles Dickens

If the Face Fits

JEFF'S PHYSICAL resemblance to the dead soldier is striking and one that is examined in detail by author Walter Semkiw, MD, in his book *Born Again* (Ritana Books, New Delhi, 2006). Dr Semkiw's theory is that we carry more than memories over from a previous life – we also bring our attitudes, talents, personal preferences, habits and physical characteristics: specifically our physiognomy (facial architecture).

Dr Semkiw claims to have matched several celebrities to their former incarnations by comparing their physical resemblance, characteristics and attributes to likely historical figures. Based on these criteria he makes a case for identifying J.K. Rowling, author of the Harry Potter books, as the most recent reincarnation of Victorian novelist Charles Dickens, movie star Halle Berry as the reincarnation of Dorothy Dandridge and talk show host Oprah Winfrey as the reincarnation of eighteenth-century orator James Wilson. Of course, such claims cannot be verified and add nothing of substance to the argument in favour of reincarnation, but the theory may be sound, that we are essentially the same personality from life to life. But Dr Semkiw's credibility is seriously undermined by the admission that he makes many of his comparisons on intuition and that these hunches are then 'confirmed' by his Egyptian spirit guide, known as Ahtun Re!

Of more interest was Dr Semkiw's idea to ask a linguistics expert, Professor Miriam Petruck of the University of California, to compare several passages in Colonel Gordon's memoirs with excerpts from official reports written by Captain Keane during his service as a fire chief.

Her findings were by no means conclusive, but she discovered that several significant grammatical features were shared by the two sets of writing. These were the frequent use of compound sentences, the use of preposed clauses in complex sentences, the use of existential sentences with negation, adverbial clauses at the beginning of a sentence and the change from active to passive voice within a single passage, which indicates that something was resolved or achieved without the intervention of those involved.

Dr Petruck, understandably, reserved judgment in this case, but the idea of comparing samples of writing with those of a person with whom the subject may be connected through a past life is one which should be more thoroughly investigated.

The Case of the Purloined Portrait

THE RAMIFICATIONS of reincarnation have been pored over by philosophers, mused upon by mediums and speculated upon by sceptical scientists, but few can have been as thorough in their investigation as Indianapolis police captain Robert Snow, whose 35 years on the force taught him to question every item of evidence and take nothing at face value. But what made Captain Snow's investigation unique was that the case he was investigating was his own.

It began in 1992 when the cynical cop was challenged to submit himself to a regression session by a police department psychologist who had been advocating the benefits of regression in child abuse cases.

'I think past-life regression is probably just people with a lot of imagination,' he told colleague Cathy Graban during a departmental social function. 'Probably just people who want to blame their problems on something they can't be held accountable for now. And besides, if it was true, then how come no one's ever proved they've lived a past life?'

Relishing a chance to convert a sceptic, Graban provided Snow with the number of an independent regression therapist, Mariellen Griffith, who was based in Bloomington, Illinois. Over the following weeks Snow found a number of pressing commitments that threatened to delay his visit to Mariellen indefinitely, but Graban would not let him off the hook so easily. When she virtually accused him of reneging on his promise he finally plucked up the courage to bite the bullet.

Sitting on a therapist's couch with his eyes closed, and having been asked to empty his mind, Snow felt self-conscious in the extreme, but he was so tired that his inner resistance just seemed to ebb away as the hypnotherapist led him into a state of deep relaxation.

'I was just tired and bored,' he later recalled. 'I was sitting with my eyes closed on a rather hard couch, and I could hear street noises out the window to my right…'

Graban regressed the middle-aged policeman to his childhood and once those images were sustainable she asked him to go back further still.

It was then, when he ceased to try to recall long forgotten events that something happened, 'something so bizarre and startling I would have screamed in surprise if I hadn't already lost my breath.'

'Something so bizarre and startling happened that I would have screamed in surprise if I hadn't lost my breath'

Graban's voice seemed to come from some distance as she invited Robert to meet his inner guide. It all seemed like so much New Age nonsense to a man who had seen the very worst of human nature, but he indulged her.

'What is he wearing?' Graban asked.

'A long white gown,' Robert replied, before he could take in the significance of what he had just said.

The images that then unfolded before him were as vivid as a movie and the fact that they had arisen spontaneously suggested that they were genuine memories as opposed to the products of Robert's imagination. They had a life of their own and could not be manipulated at will. There were scenes from several lifetimes, all of which Robert viewed through the eyes of his former selves, but the one that provided the most detail was that of a nineteenth-century portrait painter living in New York, which culminated with the painting of a hunchbacked woman.

When Robert came out of the light trance he had been put into by Graban all he could think was, 'Why would anyone with a severe deformity want to have their portrait painted?'

It seemed bizarre, but it was a significant clue to the identity of the painter whose name had not been revealed during the 'visions'. In fact there was an abundance of visual clues – 28 to be precise – which Robert was determined to verify if only to prove that regression was no more than the recollection of long-forgotten facts and impressions from a person's present life, which are mistakenly assumed to be memories of a previous incarnation. Incredibly, even after his intense experience Robert still did not believe in reincarnation!

Robert's 'inner guide' was a man in a long white gown and the images that unfolded before him were as vivid as a movie

So, with the impartiality and passion of a detective on the trail of an unknown suspect, Robert spent a year trawling through every art book he could find, visiting every art gallery in the neighbouring states and corresponding with art dealers across the country in search of the portrait of the hunchback and the artist who had painted her. All in vain.

At this point his passion was in danger of becoming an obsession and so his wife tactfully suggested that they take a vacation and travel to New Orleans, somewhere she had always wanted to go. It was there, while strolling through the French Quarter, that Robert chanced upon the portrait he had been seeking for so long, in a small private art gallery in an obscure backstreet.

> *For the next several minutes I didn't move from in front of the portrait, but instead continued closing my eyes to see again and again the scene of me painting this very portrait in my studio, and then opening my eyes to see the actual finished portrait… During my 30 years as a police officer, I have always searched for the truth. Sometimes the truth didn't turn out to be what I expected, but still, the truth was what I had always searched for. And now, here I was, seeming to be facing the truth I had been looking for, but at the same time trying to deny it, trying to find any way to deny the truth of what I had found.*

In questioning the gallery guide Robert learnt that the name of the artist was Carroll Beckwith, a minor American painter, and that the portrait had been in a private collection for many years and had never been reproduced in a book. That ruled out the possibility that Robert had seen it at some point in this life and forgotten about it. According to the guide there hadn't been an exhibition of Beckwith's work in the past 75 years because he was too obscure to arouse sufficient interest. The picture had only just been put on display in the hope of attracting a sale, a fact which raised the whole question of this fortuitous coincidence being an example of what Jung called synchronicity, Fate, or an encounter engineered by his Higher Self to force him to acknowledge that such incidents might be part of a bigger picture. But such questions were too much to take in at the time.

> *As the gallery worker's answer dashed my seemingly logical explanation for what had happened, the vertigo returned. My whole belief system was not only teetering, it was falling... And so I simply stood there open-mouthed, numb and detached from reality.*

Even in the light of this encounter, Robert did not forget his police training and continued to pursue the physical evidence of his supposed connection with Carroll Beckwith. After much research he was able to lay his hands on the diary of the artist, which had been bequeathed to one of his descendants. From this Robert claims to have been able to verify 26 of the 28 details obtained from the regression. Sufficient, one might be tempted to say, to secure a conviction in the case for reincarnation.

Curiously, it was only after the regression session that Snow rediscovered his enthusiasm for writing and finally became the author he had always wanted to be. In addition to penning the autobiographical story of his hunt for his 'former self', *Looking For Carroll Beckwith*, Snow has also published a series of true crime titles, covering issues from personal safety and family abuse to stalkers, cults and domestic terrorism. So whether the past life he recalled was really his own or not, the hypnotherapy worked. And that, after all, is surely the real benefit of regression.

The tomb is not a blind alley:
it is a thoroughfare.
It closes on the twilight.
It opens on the dawn.

Victor Hugo

VI

Regression

I know I am deathless… We have thus far exhausted trillions of winters and summers,/There are trillions ahead, and trillions ahead of them.

Walt Whitman

IT IS RELATIVELY rare for past life impressions to emerge spontaneously during our waking hours when we are preoccupied with the present and the brain is continually active. They are more likely to surface when the conscious mind has been put to sleep during periods of deep relaxation or in our dreams. Receptive states can also be induced by hypnosis and various other methods designed to access the unconscious, but unless one understands how these techniques are applied it is impossible to make a serious assessment of the memories recovered under these conditions. This section explains how regression can uncover deep-seated (or suppressed) memories and how to tell the difference between genuine memories and imagination. It also outlines the case against hypnotic regression.

✣ WHAT IS REGRESSION? ✣

CONTRARY TO POPULAR belief you do not have to be suffering from irrational fears or recurring nightmares to benefit from regression. On the contrary, most of the people who undergo regression do so because they are curious to know why their relationships appear to be following a pattern, why they encounter similar problems again and again and how they can break the habits that appear to be holding them back from realizing their full potential.

Becoming aware of a problem in a past life, such as being punished for a crime you did not commit, is the first step to overcoming its harmful effects

Not all past life memories are unpleasant and those that are can offer closure if they reveal the source of certain attitudes. For example, a solitary young man known personally to the author, who was distrustful of people in general and had cultivated few friends, discovered under hypnosis that he had been hounded by a jeering mob in a former life and that they had taunted him as he was executed for a crime he did not commit. Although the injustice could not be undone, it was sufficient for him to become

consciously aware of this incident for the resentment to be dispelled, after which he became more confident and sociable.

Past Life Regression is considered perfectly safe as long as the subject keeps their sense of perspective and does not identify with their former self to the extent that they retreat into the past – especially if there is a possibility that the recollections may be a fantasy created by the unconscious mind to compensate for a lack of identity or a sense of self-worth. The only recollections that can be taken seriously are those that arise spontaneously and which cannot be manipulated by the imagination. Genuine past life impressions will have a life of their own and will unfold like the images on a movie screen. Those that reveal details of names, places and dates which can later be verified through research should be considered worth recording in a journal, as should those that stir strong emotions. However, any images that do not ring true can be dismissed as products of the imagination – although it has to be said that they might nevertheless be significant in the same way that certain dreams can reveal concerns that the conscious mind seeks to suppress.

Needless to say, hypnosis and other regression techniques should never be practised by anyone suffering from psychological problems or under the influence of alcohol or drugs, prescribed or otherwise. If you are anxious about your fitness to try regression you should consult your doctor, therapist or counsellor.

My life often seemed to me like a story that has no beginning and no end. I had the feeling that I was an historical fragment, an excerpt for which the preceding and succeeding text was missing. I could well imagine that I might have lived in former centuries and there encountered questions I was not yet able to answer; that I had been born again because I had not fulfilled the task given to me.

Carl Jung (right)

Hypnotic Regression

AMERICAN HYPNOTHERAPIST and counsellor Jeanne Philips offers her clients hypnotic regression, but only if they request it:

Often a client who has come to me for counselling will ask to be regressed at some point during treatment because they suspect that the root of their problem lies in a past life. It is not something that I actively promote and I never try to persuade them that they need it. But if they express an eagerness to go deeper with someone they have come to trust, I can take them to a place where they feel safe and secure.

I have been regressed by some of the most eminent experts in the field. I know how traumatic it can be, but if a suppressed memory needs to be cleared then regression is the safest and most effective method of processing it. When I was regressed I re-experienced my death in the gas chamber of a Nazi concentration camp. I watched my parents suffocating before my eyes. I wasn't a mere observer. I was reliving it. But afterwards I felt I had released something that had been a burden, that had oppressed me all of my life. I lost my fear of death, my fear of abandonment and of being terrorized and bullied. Exploring past lives is part of our instinctual need to understand who we are and why we think and behave in the way we do.

We need to forgive so that we can move on. Clinging to the past and reliving a former injustice only serves to damage the individual who cannot clear it.

A good example of this was a client who would unconsciously wreck all of her relationships. She couldn't give herself fully to anyone. As a child she had suffered abuse and had been abandoned by her alcoholic mother.

Counselling wasn't enough so I regressed her to a point where she re-experienced life in the womb. At that stage she remembered that her mother had tried to commit suicide because she hadn't got

When Jeanne Philips was regressed, she re-experienced her death in the gas chamber of a Nazi concentration camp

over the loss of her first child. She heard the doctors talking about her mother's precarious mental state and the risk she was running with her second pregnancy.

She felt her mother's anguish and came out of the regression feeling sorry for her mother and realizing that her mother had blamed her for having to live through more pain.

In a subsequent session she relived a former life in which she had been the sole survivor of a massacre and had spent the remainder of her life alone in the mountains. She emerged from the regression feeling free for the first time in her life and she understood why she had difficulty relating to other people. That was enough to begin the process of healing.

The Case Against Hypnotic Regression

HYPNOSIS HAS always been viewed with a healthy dose of scepticism by the orthodox scientific community, but when practitioners claimed that it could be an effective means of recovering memories from a previous incarnation the sceptics became downright hostile. While hypnosis has been proven effective in the cure of certain phobias and addictions, critics argue that we still know very little about the nature of the unconscious mind, so there is no way of knowing if the alleged 'memories' are genuine or simply products of the subject's imagination. Subjects have been known to create convincing past lives from material taken in at a glance many years earlier, of which the conscious mind has no recollection – a condition known as hypermnesia. A long-forgotten bedtime story heard as a small child can form the basis of an elaborate fantasy extracted under hypnosis in adulthood which the subject, in all innocence, will believe to be absolutely genuine.

A long-forgotten bedtime story can form the basis of an elaborate fantasy that can be extracted under hypnosis in adulthood

A striking example of this psychological phenomenon discredited the celebrated case of American housewife Virginia Tighe who had claimed to recall a previous life as a poor Irish woman known as Bridey Murphy. Mrs Tighe's detailed accounts of life in rural Cork a hundred years earlier was headline news in the 1950s, but quickly disappeared from the front pages after a national newspaper revealed that she had been raised by an Irish nanny from whom it was thought

Henry Ford, seen here with a friend in a Model N in 1903, believed his genius to be 'the fruit of long experience in many lives'

she might have picked up crucial facts about the period, including the names of local shops and certain parochial expressions. Under hypnosis 'Bridey' had spoken of a friend called Kevin who had also lived in Cork. Digging deeper, the reporters discovered that Mrs Tighe had a childhood friend called Kevin Corkell, which seemed more than a coincidence. They also unearthed the fact that his aunt had died in the same manner as 'Bridey', by falling down the stairs, but even more telling was the fact that his mother's maiden name was none other than Bridey Murphy.

Another notable case was that of a man who recalled under hypnosis a previous life as a braggard and womanizer in the Irish Guards. His name in this earlier incarnation, he claimed, had been Timothy O'Malley and he had died in 1892 by falling from his horse. It later transpired that the subject had unconsciously identified with an enemy of his grandfather, a Brian O'Malley, who had run the old man out of Ireland and later died after falling from his horse. The theory is that the boy had unconsciously recast himself in the role of his grandfather's enemy because he had displeased his grandfather when he had borrowed the old man's horse without permission.

The most vociferous critics of hypnotic regression accuse practitioners of feeding their clients leading questions and of exploiting their subjects'

Leopold Mozart with his daughter Maria-Anna and son Wolfgang Amadeus, who believed he had inherited his gifts from a previous life

unconscious need to please their therapist. Under these conditions a client may create a fictitious past life identity which embodies a quality or characteristic that they lack in their present incarnation, a syndrome known as paramnesia.

Detractors point out that under hypnosis every subject is suggestible and cite the fact that many apparently talentless people have demonstrated considerable creativity under hypnosis although they showed no such ability in waking life. Advocates of hypnotic regression counter this by saying that such talents were learnt in a previous life and cite child prodigies such as Mozart as examples. Mozart himself believed that his gifts were carried over from a previous life.

The industrialist Henry Ford declared, 'I adopted the theory of reincarnation when I was 26. Genius is experience. Some seem to think that it is a gift or talent, but it is the fruit of long experience in many lives.'

There is no denying that the mind can play tricks, even when we are not under hypnosis, and that we are all subject to self-deception from time to time. The ego, the self-centred, immature aspect of our psyche is continually seeking to inflate our self-image and will seize on the slightest

HARRIET MARTINEAU.

opportunity to recast itself as an important person. That is why many immature individuals look to regression to give them the sense of self-worth that they have failed to attain in their present life. The mature, integrated adult has no need of this fantasy, which is not to say that they do not believe in regression or reincarnation, only that they would view any information about their former lives as something which might explain their present condition and circumstances.

We do not believe in immortality because we can prove it, but we try to prove it because we cannot help believing it.

Harriet Martineau

False Memories

THE UNCONSCIOUS MIND is as impenetrable a mystery to science as is the spirit world. Psychologists can do little more than probe around in the dark and try and make sense of the few clues and fragments they can retrieve of the bigger picture.

Finnish psychiatrist Dr Reima Kampman demonstrated the extent to which individuals can unconsciously adopt another person's history as their own when he published the results of a series of experiments he had conducted in the 1960s. Under hypnosis a teenage girl 'recalled' a previous life as a boy whose father was a ship's captain named Aitmatov. The girl gave a vivid description of her lonely life following the death of her father who had drowned in Lake Issykjokul.

Curiously, the girl remembered nothing of her former life after she had been brought back to waking consciousness. It was only after a subsequent regression that Dr Kampman identified the source of these memories. It transpired that many years earlier she had read a novel called *The White Ship*, which was set around Lake Issykjokul and featured a lonely little boy who drowned himself in similar circumstances. The author's name was Aitmatov.

Another example was that of a nineteen-year-old girl who described her life as an English inn-keeper's daughter during the Middle Ages. She even recalled a popular song of the period while under hypnosis which was later confirmed as authentic, as was the dialect she had sung it in. It seemed to be a clear case of past life recollection. Again, she had no memory of this after returning to waking consciousness.

Under hypnosis, one girl described her life as an inn-keeper's daughter in the Middle Ages. She even recalled a popular song of the period

It was only when Dr Kampman regressed her a second time that the girl recalled the day she had leafed through a book on the history of music by composer Benjamin Britten and Imogen Holst. Kampman was able to locate the book and confirm that the song was included, rendered in a simplified form of medieval English that his subject had never studied.

✣ Other Techniques ✣

ALTHOUGH HYPNOTIC regression is the most common method for recovering past life recollections, there are several equally effective techniques, some of which can be safely practised without supervision.

Journaling is a variation on the free association exercises used by psychoanalysts to tease out clues from a patient's subconscious.

Subjects are encouraged to keep a diary recording the details of their most vivid dreams, or their thoughts on a period or place to which they are attracted.

The first time they do the exercise they are asked to choose from one of these dreams or descriptions and write the first word or phrase that comes

into their mind in connection with it in the centre of the page. Then they circle it. Next, they draw a line from this to the left side margin where they must write the next word or phrase that comes into their mind and circle this. Then they draw another line to the opposite side of the paper where they write a word or phrase associated with the word in the second bubble and so on until they have covered the page in a web of encircled clues. At first there may not seem to be a connection between the words but if the exercise has been done at speed, with no time to think about what they are writing, they may have produced a trail of clues to a past life which can provide material for further research.

Dialoguing is another method that promises results if it is undertaken seriously. For this exercise a character is chosen from a significant dream and the individual concerned engages in a written dialogue with this personality, who may be from their past or who may be another aspect of their own psyche. Again, it is crucial that the person writes the first thing that comes into their mind regardless of whether it makes any sense to them. If they persevere there will be a breakthrough, after which the words will flow from their pen before they can think of them. The resulting 'script' should be extremely revealing.

Even more effective, potentially, is the technique known as Storytelling, which involves selecting key words or phrases from a vivid dream, or images associated with the period or place which the person suspects may be significant, and using them as the basis of a story. The key is to allow the story to unfold without conscious effort, and the characters to speak through the dialogue without analyzing their possible significance, until the 'story' has come to its natural conclusion. Many repressed memories have resurfaced using this method because it allows the subject to recall what may be a traumatic episode with the detachment of an observer and, of course, it does not necessitate hypnosis, of which some subjects are wary.

As with all methods of psychoanalysis it is rare to make a breakthrough on the first try. Patience and persistence are required to break through the barriers of self-censorship erected by the conscious mind, which does not easily allow the casually curious to access the unconscious.

It is nature's kindness that we do not remember past births. Life would be a burden if we carried such a tremendous load of memories.

Mohandas K. Gandhi

'Patience and persistence are required to break through the barriers of self-censorship erected by the conscious mind'

✣ Inherited Memory ✣

THOSE LOOKING FOR what they would consider to be a rational explanation for regression phenomena frequently argue in favour of the theory of inherited memory. This states that we all inherit more than merely physical characteristics from our ancestors – we also assimilate their genetic memory. For example, the descendants of a persecuted people might be inclined to distrust anyone who is not of their racial or religious group and might recall being burned as a heretic, or tortured by their enemies, as if they themselves had experienced these events in a previous life. Closed communities and societies with a specific identity would also pass on their attitudes and the sum of their collective experience, simply because of their shared background and beliefs.

This notion of the existence of an archetypal memory is offered as an explanation for such remarkable events as the child prophets of Cevennes who preached Protestant sermons in France during the seventeenth century, even before they could speak fluently, and the high incidence of young Jewish children who are haunted by nightmares of the Holocaust, even though their parents would have shielded them from knowledge of the event because of their tender age.

Such experiences may seem vividly real to the person who dreams them night after night, or who is confronted by them during regression, but psychologists might argue that such images are merely symbolic of the

If we recall a previous incarnation as a heroic figure, we may be unconsciously compensating for qualities we lack

subject's state of mind. The fear of being ostracized by society and cold-shouldered by our friends is something that worries us all at one time or another in our lives and such 'memories' may be manufactured by the unconscious to express those anxieties. Conversely, if we recall a previous incarnation as a heroic figure, or someone whose character or circumstances are in stark contrast to our own, we may be unknowingly creating a past life to compensate for qualities we believe we lack in our present personality. However, this conflicts with the countless cases in which people recall the details of very mundane lives.

A more likely explanation is that the unconscious mind may invent a traumatic previous existence to explain a patient's present neurosis. The person who eats to excess might retreat into a fabricated past life in which they starved to death in order to excuse their over-indulgence in the present. Or they might rationalize their fears by claiming that they originate in a former incarnation. This may of course be true, but regression therapy was designed to cure sufferers of irrational inhibitions and phobias, not justify them.

The important point, though, is that when treating a patient with a neurosis psychotherapists do not need to believe in reincarnation. It is sufficient that the patient believes that the 'memory' is genuine because it provides an explanation for their fear and that in itself is enough to effect a cure.

The person who eats to excess might retreat into a fabricated past life in which they starved to death to excuse their overindulgence

✤ Woolger: Healing the Past ✤

ROGER J. WOOLGER, Ph.D., is a British-born Jungian analyst, regression therapist and professional lecturer with degrees in psychology, religion and philosophy from Oxford and London Universities. His first book, *Other Lives Other Selves* (Doubleday, 1987), is an innovative synthesis of Jungian depth psychology, bodywork, yoga psychology, psychodrama and Eastern meditation principles. It is widely regarded as the definitive work in the field of regression therapy, together with its companion book *Healing Your Past Lives* (2004), which integrates aspects of Tibetan Buddhism and shamanism. In the last decade, his work has evolved into the highly original therapeutic tool he calls Deep Memory Process™, which he has discussed and demonstrated on American, Canadian and Italian network television. He currently runs training programmes for therapists in North America and Britain.

The following extracts are taken from a lecture given by Woolger to the 1998 Conference of the Association of Humanistic Psychology and 'Eternal Return', an unpublished manuscript published here for the first time with the permission of the author.

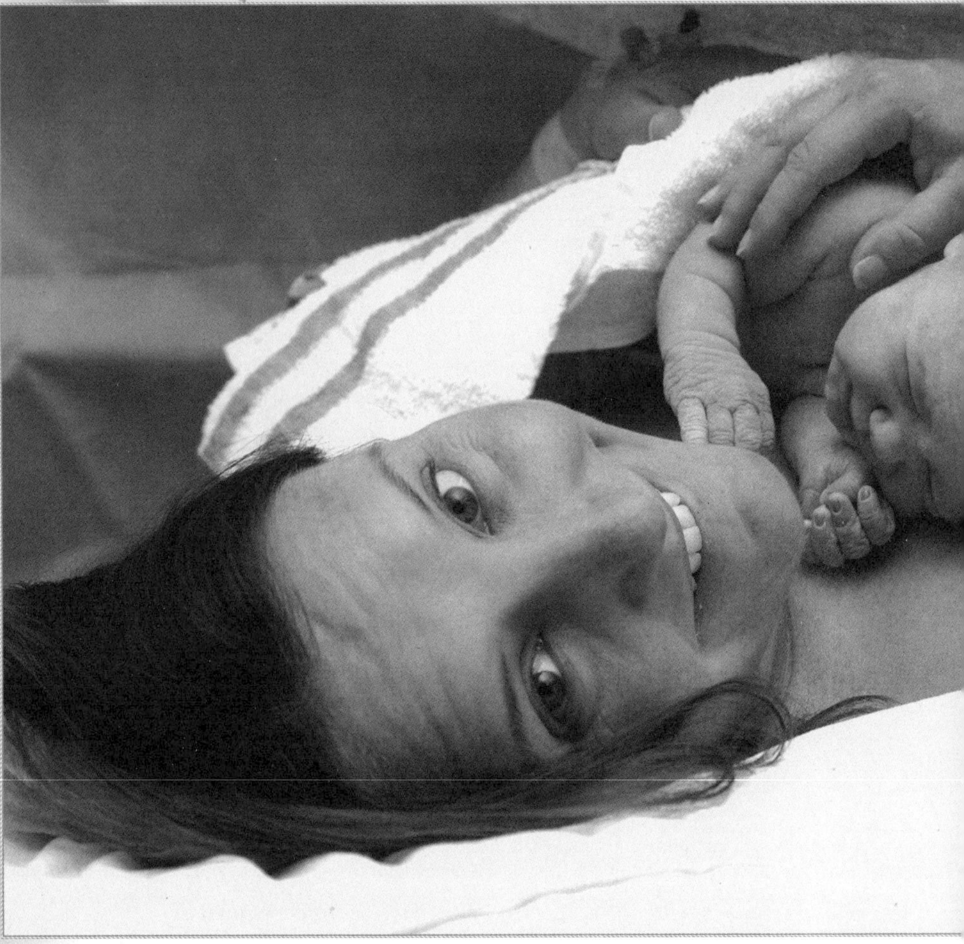

As Thomas Verney incontrovertibly showed, it is possible for a person under hypnosis to remember what happened during their birth

How is it possible to Remember Past Lives? A Reply to the Sceptics

WORKING WITH PAST life images and allowing them to unfold into scenes and stories is essentially a meditative process. It requires a stillness, a certain trust in the creative powers of the deep imagination as well as a readiness to encounter not just appealing but often dark and disturbing images.

Many people object to the idea of past life recall by saying, 'This is all nonsense. We know scientifically that the mind of an infant at birth is empty. Its neurones haven't developed yet. How can it possibly remember previous lifetimes?'

Others object: 'This is all imagination, just fantasy. These clients of yours are making up these stories to please you as a therapist. And in any case it's

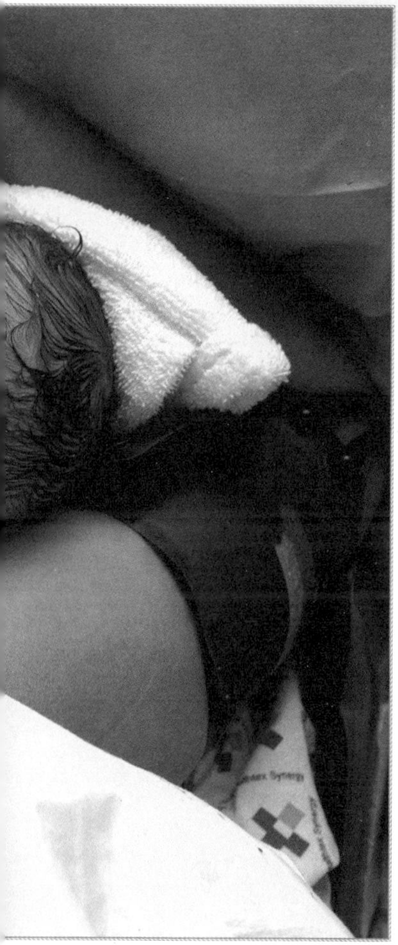

quite fashionable to have past lives these days.'

In over twenty years of regressing people, I have found cryptamnesia [false memory syndrome] to be a relatively rare phenomenon. The majority of past life memories are not reproducing novels and films. Not even American television would dare come up with the huge number of mundane and unglamorous stories we hear so often! In fact, if I were to produce a thousand cases from my own files and from those of colleagues, I would be willing to bet that only two or three per cent of this sample could actually be traced to any known novel, TV show or Hollywood movie.

The third common objection to past-life memories is the idea that the mind of the infant has not matured enough physiologically to provide a neuronal basis for memory... the idea that the infant cannot remember has been challenged in recent years. There is a huge body of evidence from research with hypnotic regression collected by Thomas Verney in his classic book *The Secret Life of the Unborn Child* which shows incontrovertibly how it is possible for a person under hypnosis to remember exactly what happens at birth, *in utero* and even all the way back to conception. It is now widely accepted by experts in this field that there is some degree of proto-consciousness in the foetal being that records and overhears whatever the mother is talking and thinking about. Foetal consciousness is telepathically bound to that of the mother in other words.

The trouble with the *tabula rasa* [blank slate] theory is that it assumes that memory is somehow stored at the physical level and that there is no other way for it to be stored. I believe this to be a fundamental metaphysical error deriving from the fallacious premise that consciousness is contained in the brain...

After a lifetime of research into brain physiology and having asked all the questions that could be asked about the body-mind interaction [the British

neurologist] Sir John Eccles stated unequivocally his belief that the mind is simply of a different order than the physical world and that you would never find evidence of mind in the brain. Mind interacts with the brain, but it does not belong to the same reality. It's about as useless to look in the brain for mind as it is to look for music by carving holes in your CD recording. 'In' is a spatial metaphor that does not refer to physical space.

Some years ago, following an important hint from *The Tibetan Book of the Dead*, I started during regression work to look very carefully at what people were going through at the moment that they were dying in a past life. I found that the death experience and the way people clung to death or died with despairing thoughts had a huge amount to say about their general attitudes to life in their current lives.

Typical thoughts that have come out of regressions at the moment of death... *they didn't want me... they abandoned me* – these are children who have been put out to die abandoned, lost in some kind of attack, and so on. *I've had to do it all alone*, say people who are left to struggle or die alone. People who died in a famine say that there wasn't enough, there was never enough. People who are killed for speaking out or saying something they shouldn't have done say: *'I should have kept silent... I should have kept it to myself.'*

Typical thoughts that have come out of regressions at the moment of death include: 'they didn't want me... they abandoned me'

Others are guilty: *I could have done more... it's all my fault... I didn't do enough.* Vengeful thoughts include *I'll get back at them*, or there may be negative thoughts about the self: *I'm hopeless... it's useless... I'm disgusting*, or *I'll never be able to do this again... I'll never walk again... I'm trapped... I'll never get out of this.* Following betrayals some say: *'It's not safe to show what I really feel... people will let you down... it's all hopeless.'* Such thoughts arise in past life sessions where people have remembered dying in despair or in hopeless situations.

I worked with a woman not long ago who had difficulty entering into a past life. All she could see was a roadway beneath her and buildings that looked as if they had been bombed. When I got her to look more closely she saw what looked like convoys of vehicles that had also been bombed.

As she is describing this, sitting in a chair, she goes absolutely rigid. I said to her, 'What's your body trying to do?' and she said, 'I don't know, but I've got to hold on tight.'

As we explored the subtle body memory it became clearer and clearer that she was holding a steering wheel and she had her foot on a brake. Slowly we pieced together the fact that she had been a German soldier in a convoy that had been bombed by fighter planes. The soldier had died instantly, anxiously trying to stop the car and escape the bombing, but it was not a conscious death at all. Many experiences are like this: fragmentary, confused and frozen. By bringing the outside consciousness of the therapist into the story, we can usually help release the soul fragment.'

Very frequently the portal or doorway into a past life memory is a disturbing event in our present life that awakens an older memory. Roger recalls an experience he shared with a young woman in California who had come to a workshop because she had been traumatized by the memory of a recent car accident. She had come across an overturned vehicle and being a trained nurse she had approached the wreck expecting to help the injured. But when she saw a baby's bottle lying on the back seat she 'freaked' and fled the scene after informing the police.

> *Just the thought of a dead baby had taken her through a window into another lifetime*

All I did was have her focus on that moment when she had seen the baby bottle and had 'freaked out', Roger recalls.

I said to her, 'What does that baby bottle make you think of?'

And she said, 'I was too late.'

I said gently, 'Go on!'

She said, 'I was too late to save the baby.'

And I simply said to her, 'Repeat that phrase a few times and see where it takes you.'

She said, 'It's too late, it's too late. Oh my God, the baby's dead.'

'Where are you?' I asked Sally.

Sally sees herself on a mountainside in Scotland. She immediately feels she has the stocky body of a Scottish peasant woman who is up tending the sheep and she's heard gunfire in the little village where she lives. It's the seventeenth century, when there are violent skirmishes between the English and the Scots border people. She comes running down the hill, bursts into the little cottage and there is her sister and two babies, hers and her sister's all shot, all dead.

'I was too late,' she said, 'I should have been there for my child. It was all my fault.'

Just the thought of a dead baby had taken her through a window into another lifetime. The transition was almost instant when I invited her to

She had come across an overturned vehicle, and 'freaked' when she saw a baby's bottle on the back seat

focus. When she'd first been triggered, she was too upset to stay with the process, but the images were right there close to the surface. It simply took a stepping through that doorway to find herself in another lifetime. It was a painful one to remember, but it helped her understand why in this lifetime she had chosen not to have children. Eventually, she was able to forgive herself for the failure in the past life and look much more favorably at the

possibility maybe of relationships and a family by the time the workshop and our sessions together were over.

Often the releasing of trauma… is like peeling skins from an onion. In other words, not only must we posit that the psyche is multidimensional but that the sufferings of the soul exist in a variety of subtle forms not restricted to the gross body or the immediate constraints of time and space. Such awareness, difficult as it is for the materialist to grasp, may take us into surprising depths – and heights – within the psyche. Compared to the great psycho-spiritual disciplines of the East, Western psychotherapy is still in its infancy and is still learning to work with other dimensions of the soul such as residues of previous lives, ancestral memories or the influence of spiritual healing from other realms. And like much uncharted territory we would be wise to regard most maps and reports as purely provisional, and remain open to making constant revisions as new vistas open up.

I am certain that I have been here as
I am now a thousand times before, and
I hope to return a thousand times.

Thomas Huxley

Live so that thou mayest desire
to live again – that is thy duty
– for in any case thou wilt
live again!

Friedrich Nietzsche
(left)

VII

Through a Glass Darkly: Psychic Readings

The sceptic who refutes the fact of another existence beyond death and leaves a demonstration with nothing but scorn for mediumship may be the person holding the greatest fear of dying.

Stephen O'Brien,
Visions of Another World

IF YOU DON'T want to subject yourself to a regression session, you will be delighted to hear that there is a good, viable alternative – a past life 'reading' with a psychic. Many specialize in recovering impressions from their client's former lives by reading their aura, the radiance of etheric energy which surrounds every human being. Some of the readings detailed in the following pages provide the most compelling evidence for the belief in reincarnation on record, but even more incredible are the vivid recollections experienced by the psychics themselves. This section includes public figures, past and present, who were brave enough to declare their belief in reincarnation despite fear of ridicule, as well as the remarkable past lives of singer Elton John, which range from French aristocrat to humble footslogger in World War I.

171646

✤ PUBLIC FIGURES AND ✤ REINCARNATION

PUBLIC FIGURES have a lot to lose by declaring their belief in reincarnation. They can open themselves to ridicule and by doing so damage their reputation and credibility.

Opposite: General George S. Patton; below: 55BC and Roman legionaries fight their way ashore in Britain

General Patton

NO ONE COULD accuse General George S. Patton of being a fantasist, yet 'Old Blood and Guts', as they called him, had no qualms about sharing his belief in reincarnation with the men under his command. Patton was convinced that his tactical skills had been acquired in earlier campaigns, the first with Alexander the Great at the battle of Tyre, again in the Hundred Years' War between England and France (1337–1453) and finally under Napoleon. Patton was so taken with the idea that he even wrote a poem:

Through the travail of the ages,
Midst the pomp and toil of war,
Have I fought and strove and perished,
Countless times upon this star.
So as through a glass, and darkly
The age long strife I see
Where I fought in many guises,
Many names, – but always me.

In December 1917 the young Patton had politely declined an offer of a tour of the French town of Langres where he had been billeted by assuring his escort that he had been there before and knew it well. Instead, he took the officer on a tour of the Roman encampment, pointing out the site of the amphitheatre, the temples, the drill ground and the forum where he had lived as one of Julius Caesar's legionaries.

During the Second World War, in response to a British general who observed that he would have made a great marshal in Napoleon's army had he lived in the nineteenth century, Patton casually replied, 'But I did.'

Celebrities and Reincarnation

Friends are all souls that we've known in other lives. We're drawn to each other. Even if I have only known them a day it doesn't matter... we must have met somewhere before....

George Harrison

The Beatles believed in reincarnation. John Lennon once said, 'I imagine death is like getting out of one car and climbing into another'

CELEBRITIES ARE generally thought to be fair game for ridicule and many openly invite it, but it takes a certain type of courage to publicly admit your belief in reincarnation when you know that many of your

admirers may never look at you in the same adoring light again.

Among those who have done so recently are Sylvester Stallone, who is convinced that he died a gruesome death in the French Revolution; Tina Turner, who was told by a psychic that she had been the Egyptian queen Hatshepsut; John Travolta, who has accepted the possibility that he was probably Rudolph Valentino the last time round; and actress Shirley MacLaine, who believes that she has been an Egyptian handmaiden, an artist's model in eighteenth century Paris and an inhabitant of the lost continent of Atlantis.

In one of her past lives, actress Shirley MacLaine believes that she was an inhabitant of the lost continent of Atlantis

Aliens and Atlantis

ANY MENTION of former lives in Atlantis is guaranteed to invoke howls of derision from the cynics and groans from those who argue for an objective study of the evidence in favour of reincarnation. Talk of Atlantis and former lives on other planets only detracts from the real issues raised by the insights gained from regression and the recollection of former lives, by means of which we are enabled to determine the purpose of our present life and gain an understanding of our true nature.

But there is always the risk that when one explores a subject that involves probing the unconscious and filtering impressions through the imagination it will inevitably elicit statements of this nature from those who cannot distinguish between fantasy and reality. No doubt some of those who make such claims are sincere in their beliefs, but any serious, objective investigation into something that cannot be proven scientifically needs to begin with case studies that can be verified.

No proof is necessary, but it helps!

LEE EVERETT, author of *Celebrity Regressions* and former wife of the late DJ and comedian Kenny Everett, had an unshakable conviction from childhood that she had lived many lives, but it was not until she actually 'saw' her former self that her new-found insights had a real and lasting impact on her life:

I had seen things others didn't see and I found myself talking about past lives as if it was the most natural thing in the world

> *I didn't need proof of past lives. I was born believing. But I couldn't share my psychic and spiritual experiences with my parents because they didn't believe. I had seen things that others didn't see and I found myself talking about my past lives as if it was the most natural thing in the world. It wasn't until I was old enough to go to school that I realized the other children thought I was nuts for even mentioning these things.*

But believing was not enough to cure Kenny, who suffered from recurring and debilitating depressions during the early years of their marriage. In desperation, Lee went along to a spiritualist church and was told by a medium that she would soon find a book that would help cure him. Lee was sceptical, because the last thing she needed was a book. She was looking for a cure. The next day she was so exhausted that she did not leave her husband's regular prescription for sleeping pills with the pharmacist as normal but waited in the shop until it was dispensed. While she was doing so a book caught her eye.

She bought it and Kenny read it through in one sitting. From it he learnt that the cumulative side-effect of the pills was depression. From that day on he refused to take the medication and his black moods never returned. Better still, his whole nature changed for the better. The 'miracle cure' she had been praying for now inspired her to join a healing group so that she could repay the debt she felt she owed to whatever power had answered her prayer. But if she had expected to enjoy a blissful meditation, she was in for a rude awakening.

> *While I was meditating in the circle I saw with my inner eye the figure of a Catholic nun appear behind me as I went deeper and deeper into*

myself. After that I began to suffer from acute pains in the shoulder behind which she had appeared. It spread to my hands which curled so badly that surgeons persuaded me to have my carpal tunnels removed which caused me a lot of discomfort and all for nothing! The pain did not go away. I consulted every conventional medical practitioner and complementary therapist I could find, but none of them had any idea what was happening to me. One doctor diagnosed it as rheumatoid arthritis and prescribed a course of increasingly powerful drugs which I would have been on for the rest of my life, but I feared the side-effects and besides, I knew it was nothing of the sort. I had come to the realization that it was the pain from having awoken that aspect of my personality.

Eventually in desperation I went to a psychic who told me that I had been that nun in a former life and had been tortured by the Inquisition. With that knowledge came the relief from the pain as that memory and all the emotions associated with it were released. My fingers straightened and the crippling arthritis never returned. I'm glad that I had tried all the conventional avenues first though as I had to prove to myself that there was no chance that it was a physical complaint.

From that and other experiences I learnt that it is not necessarily the trauma that we clear when we recall or relive a past life. The pain and emotion we sometimes experience come as a consequence of reconnecting with that aspect of our personality, in the same way that meeting an old friend might rekindle suppressed emotions. The pain is not the point. It only reminds you who you were so you can discover who you really are. We are all composites of the various personalities we have been through all our lives.

Above: 'a Catholic nun appeared to me as I went deeper and deeper into myself'; below: the Inquisition goes about its business

It is not true though that it is only painful memories that are recalled during regression or a psychic reading. Most of the time the memories are monotonously

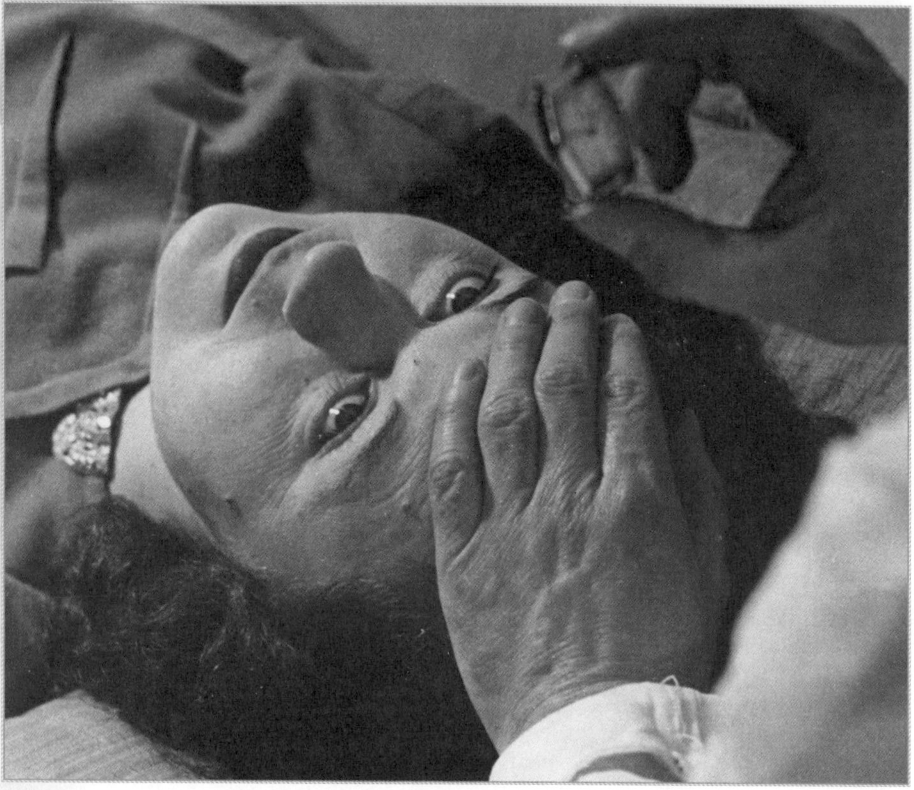

Hypnotic regression (above) only reawakens the memory, whereas spiritual regression has the potential to provide a deep sense of peace

mundane and seriously boring. That might disappoint someone who comes hoping to be told that they were a significant historical figure in a former life, but I am not here to provide proof, only to heal. I don't put them in a trance or lead them in any way. I simply ask them to visualize a door, a staircase or a house to get them focused and then ask them to enter the picture and explore. I will only ask them to look in the wardrobe to discover if they are male or female or to look in the mirror. I'll ask them to look down at their shoes to see what they are wearing and help identify the period. I'll also ask them where they eat in the hope that it will draw them to the dining room where we might meet other members of the family. But it is their memory that is released not mine.

Regression is not dangerous but it should never be attempted alone. You need the support of someone with considerable experience to help deal with the emotional stuff that is dredged up and to take that former aspect of yourself into the light. That is the important difference between spiritual regression and hypnotic regression, which only reawakens the memory. It concentrates on the mind in isolation from the spirit. Many of my clients have commented that they have actually seen the room grow brighter at this point, or have felt a profound sense of peace.

You wouldn't think of trying to psychoanalyze yourself or give yourself counselling if you were under stress so why risk trying to regress yourself to a former life when you have no idea what you might have to face. If the incidents of frayed nerves and road rage and so on are any indication it would seem that few of us are capable of dealing with the pressures of daily life so it would be dangerous to attempt to go deep into your past life without a qualified person to help you through it.

In my opinion, the problem with regression, and hypnotic regression in particular, is that people are so easily led. And they make assumptions that fit into their personal belief system. It is very dangerous to generalize. Often some of the things you might see in a dream or vision – for want of a better word – are symbolic of a state of mind and are not to be taken literally. And of course, everyone wants to be told that they were someone special in a former life because that makes them feel special in this life. But that is not the purpose of past-life readings or regressions. For me the key word is 'clearing'. Without it someone can literally be living in the past. When you die you only take with you what you learnt, not how you learnt it. I don't use a specific technique. I just go off somewhere in meditation with the client and share their experience through what appears to be a form of heightened empathy. It is not a psychic ability but merely an acute sensitivity to an aspect of themselves that they are not consciously aware of.

The reason I chose to work with celebrities at one point was partly because I knew many of them personally but also because I wanted to introduce the subject of past lives to a wider public and didn't want to preach to the converted. Even before I met them I could tell which of them couldn't let go of their former lives by their dress and manner. Several are still acting out those roles, but only the ones they liked!

I was also excited by the prospect of working with people who did not believe such as Elton John. He was a hardened sceptic when I talked to him initially but like everyone else featured in my book he asked to come back for another session when it was over. I didn't lead them or guide them in any way. I simply acted as a facilitator, helping them to relax and talking them through it. I'll start by saying something like 'Let's go back to the day before you died. Now describe to me what you can see and sense.'

They didn't need convincing that what they had seen in their mind was real. The images were so vivid and the sensations so real that there was no room for doubt. It made them realize that when you die you don't just dry up and blow away.

'Elton John was reluctant at first to submit to regression as he believed that his present life was to be his first and last'

But it is important to remember that even though we are the product of our past actions, we cannot use whatever happened in the past as an excuse for our behaviour in the present. It is not right to say, 'I can't help being this way because such and such happened in a past life.'

That is avoiding responsibility and ignoring the fact that we all have free will and the power to make the choices that determine the course of our present life. We are not puppets at the whim of Fate. No one is holding us back from having what we want in this life. Only we can do that by imposing limitations on ourselves, some of which will be the fear of repeating past mistakes from former lives. But no choice we make is really a mistake as we learn from all our actions.

Elton John

ELTON WAS RELUCTANT at first to submit to regression as he believed that his present life was to be his first and last, but he was finally persuaded to have a go by a mutual friend, the tennis star Billie Jean King. The session took place in a villa in Acapulco, Mexico, where the three friends were sharing a Christmas vacation. Within a few minutes the flamboyant rock star was uncharacteristically subdued and speaking in a low, calm voice. Elton described what he saw:

I'm greeted in a dark, sombre hallway by a small shaggy dog. It's a dark, stone house with a very big hall. The stonework is very old, the place is cold and dreary. I really don't like it here at all.

The dining room has a long wooden table, a fireplace, and the walls are all stone. This room is very large and there are two or three people in the room. I can't make them out very well, but they're wearing very old clothes, velvets, it looks pre-Elizabethan. The woman is wearing a long dress.

It's not a poor house, it's very big but there are no ornaments of any kind. I'm now sitting in the centre, at the side of the dining table. There's a man at the head of the table – I think he's my father – and another man on my left and the woman is sitting opposite me and I feel she is my mother. We are being served food by two women wearing aprons.

I can't see the stairs but I am now in the upper part of the house in a small bedroom with a fireplace and a window, again very bare. There's a bed and a table with a candle on it. I'm wearing long, skin boots on my small feet, and a long shirt.

I'm a boy of about eight years old. It's a cold, lonely life, and I die very young, there are no more memories past this point.'

Lee guided him on to the next life, which proved to be considerably more comfortable and contained a clue to his present tastes and talents.

Elton John found himself in a beautiful French château 'lavish and crammed full of beautiful things and with gold leaf all over the place'

I'm standing in a garden looking at a beautiful French château surrounded by fields. It's my house. I enter through a magnificent wooden door with gold trim. It's an ornate house with gold leaf all over the place. I take hold of the door handle with a gloved hand. I'm a twenty-eight-year-old man, very finely dressed, rather like a cavalier, with long, curly hair, a large hat and belt with buckle and sword. The house is lavish and crammed full of beautiful things. There are paintings of the family: my mother and father and a separate one of me. The hallway is light, very light, it's full of beauty and I'm obviously wealthy. The gardens are laid out in symmetrical detail. It's a typical French Château.

There's a long dining table (not nearly as long as the first one I saw though). It seats about sixteen people on gold chairs. I can't see anyone else,

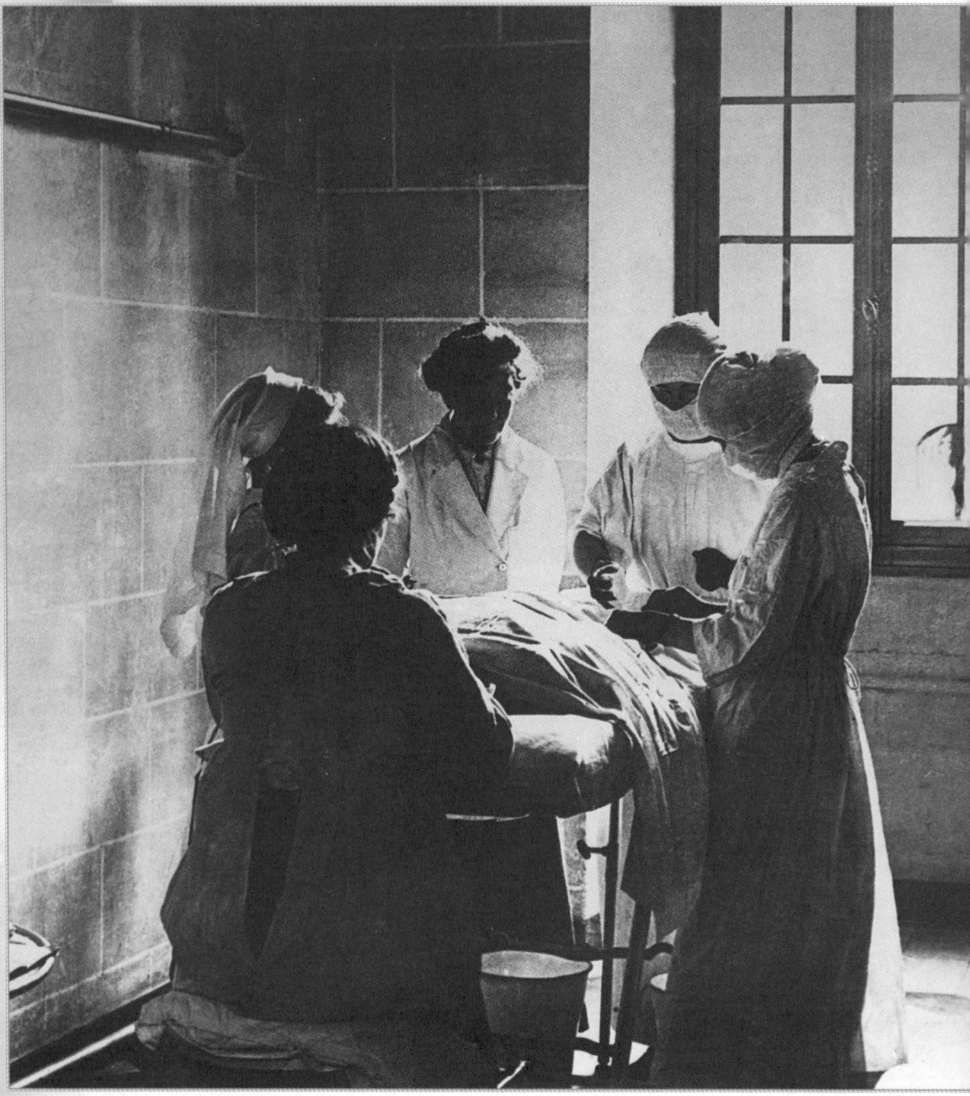

Elton John found himself being treated for shrapnel wounds during the First World War. His wife was by the bed and he was done with fighting

I seem to be eating alone. I'm being served by a young footman who brings me wine and a bird, a game bird.

Now I'm sitting in a beautiful, beautiful room with a piano. I'm alone and sitting at the piano playing. I'm not writing or reading music; I know it's my own composition.

I socialize a lot in Paris. I see myself eating a meal in a restaurant. There are six people including myself, all wearing similar clothing, late eighteenth century, fine and ornate, and we are all wearing wigs. We are just six men at

the table, no ladies, though there are ladies in the restaurant. We are talking and laughing and being very loud.

I'm now seeing myself in my early forties. I'm in Venice and I'm very ill. I'm looking out across the bay to the other side of Venice and I know I'm gravely ill. This is the hour before my death. There's a priest by my bed.

But just as Lee was expecting Elton to emerge from the vision he went on to the next without any encouragement from her. It was in stark contrast to his previous incarnation.

He saw himself as a British soldier in France during the First World War, living in the trenches and up to his ankles in filth. His khaki uniform and boots were caked in mud. The scene changed to the next day when he saw himself and the rest of his battalion trudging along a road towards a deserted farmhouse. Everyone on the march was exhausted and flopped down inside the bombed-out building, grateful for the chance to rest. The next scene appears to be about a year later.

I'm in hospital. I've been injured, there's shrapnel in my leg and I'm here to have it taken out. My wife's at the bedside. She's a small, dark-haired woman, she's only about twenty-three. The war is over for me now.

Lee takes him on to a scene from later in that life.

I'm a bus driver in London. It seems to be the early Forties. I'm living in the same small, terraced house that I was born and brought up in. The wife and I live with my parents, we have no children.

And finally, on to the last moments of that life:

I'm aged about forty now. I'm driving the bus. I've lost control and it crashes. Everything's gone dark.

That was the end of the session but it was not, evidently, the end of Elton's connection with the more creative of his former selves. That night he awoke with a tune in his head and tried to find someone in the villa who was awake, so he could play it to them, but they were all fast asleep. He went back to bed but awoke a little while later still with that same melody on his mind, so he wrote it down this time and it can now be heard on the album appropriately titled *Sleeping With The Past.* Interestingly, he has never learnt to drive.

Brian May

Brian May's regression session took place amid constant noise from ringing telephones and traffic, but links with the past were still achieved

LEE'S REGRESSION SESSION with Queen guitarist Brian May took place in the group's management offices in London's Notting Hill Gate, amidst constantly ringing telephones and traffic noise. But despite the distractions she managed to uncover a link between Brian and his present partner actress Anita Dobson, star of BBC's long-running soap *EastEnders*:

I am seeing a very light reddish-coloured wooden door with two large panels at the top and two smaller ones below. As I reach out my hand to open the door I see that it's a bit more hairy than my present hand. I am wearing a tweedy jacket and brown trousers with black, shiny, pointed shoes. Inside the room there are pictures on the wall with gilt frames, mostly landscapes. It's a big sitting room with sofas and lots of people all standing around drinking cocktails. They are all dressed quite smartly, smarter than I am. I think I am just visiting. I realize now that it's a funeral that I'm attending. I live in an end-of-terrace house in the early twentieth century. The dining room has quite a big table. There's a lady sitting there with slightly greying hair, a gentle lady. I'm quite old; I feel she is my wife. There's just her and me now – it feels like everyone else is gone.

Lee then took him back to his adolescence.

I live in a big house and my parents are quite jolly-looking. Dad's wearing a brown suit with a fob watch. It feels like 1860. I think my dad is a photographer. My first job is working outside on a farm, where there are pigs and cows. I don't like it very much. I feel like I want to get away.

By the time I'm twenty I'm apprenticed to what seems to be a solicitor – I'm learning a trade. I get married at what looks like Clapham Common: it's a church on a big green. I can't see my wife though… I can see her now: she's very beautiful, soft and warm.

She's very young, about eighteen, but very beautiful with a straight nose. Our first married home seems to be the terraced house I first saw. By the time I'm thirty we have three children. I'm still at the same job in the city at the same office. I think I'm a solicitor or something.

Brian May and his wife Anita: during the session Brian witnessed his own funeral and, back in the light, was later reunited with Anita

She then took him forward to late middle age.

I'm in the small house in the study, sitting behind a desk. I've received a piece of paper that is telling me what is happening. Someone has died and they are a long way away, in India or somewhere. I don't know who it is because I can't sort of feel anything. It feels like it's professionally important. A year later we are living in the big house; we moved into it after the news of the death of my business partner. It feels big and empty and I don't feel I've enough furniture to fill it. I feel we didn't want to move out of our lovely terraced house.

Then, it was back to the opening scene. Whose funeral was it?

I realize now it's my own. I'm seeing it all, looking at all the guests, it's very strange.

Finally, she leads him into the light where he is reunited with his wife from that lifetime. Her face changes. Brian falls silent. What is he seeing?

It's Anita, she now looks like Anita.

Street Psychic

37-YEAR-OLD BRITISH medium Tony Stockwell, star of the TV series *Street Psychic*, and author of two fascinating autobiographies, was given a unique insight into his previous incarnations when he was just seventeen. One night he 'awoke' to find himself sitting next to his sleeping self in the bed. There was no reason for fear. He was evidently having another out-of-body experience, but this one was unlike any he had experienced before. He was excited by the realization that he could float free of his body and explore the house, but as he drifted as light as a bubble out into the hall he was amazed to see an orange glow illuminating the top of the stairs. There in the centre of this unearthly light sat a fourteen-year-old boy, dressed in the saffron robes of a Tibetan monk, his legs crossed and his head shaved.

Tony Stockwell awoke one night to find that he was sitting next to his sleeping self on the bed. He found he could float free of his body and explore the house

The boy's serene expression and the energy that radiated from him put Tony at his ease and he willingly sat on the stairs at the feet of this vision, awaiting the message he intuitively knew he would be given.

After some moments of blissful silence the boy spoke, 'You have lived a

life of comparative luxury,' he said softly, 'but this has not always been the case.'

With that he stretched out an arm to show Tony a wooden bowl containing the simple food that a novice monk would eat. The boy then told Tony that in a previous life they had once been novice monks together in Tibet and he went into detail about the places they had visited and the experiences they had shared. He ended by confirming what Tony had suspected for many years, that he had been born this time around with a psychic sensitivity which the spirit world hoped he would use to bring comfort to the grieving and guidance to those who asked for his help. His parting words were those of a stern but loving parent – Tony was to do as he was told by the spirits and pass on the messages they needed to send.

Stockwell found he had lived an earlier life as a monk and had perished in an avalanche along with Zintar, his spirit guide

The next moment Tony found himself back in bed and wide awake. He was eagerly writing down a detailed description of his experience to ensure that he would never forget it. A short while later the boy communicated a second time with Tony, but this time through a friend who was also a medium. He identified himself as Zintar and described their earlier life in Tibet in greater detail, which confirmed the events Tony had seen in dreams and visions over many years. The two friends had died in an avalanche, but now they were to be reunited in this life with Tony as the medium and Zintar as his spirit guide. To this day the pair work together to bring messages of hope from the spirit world, with Zintar speaking through Tony when the latter goes into trance.

But even psychics can be sceptical when it comes to accepting evidence of their past lives and at the age of twenty-one Tony felt the need to consult a regression therapist to validate the visions he had been having since the age of five.

During childhood Tony had a recurring memory of life as an Egyptian youth named Yem who had been poisoned by an ambitious uncle. The most vivid of these 'memories' involved the slow death of this seventeen-year-old boy, who had been paralyzed by the poison and whose last days were spent lying prostrate on a slab while being tended by servant women in long black robes.

When it came to the regression session, Tony immediately returned to that lifetime and under the guidance of the hypnotherapist he began by recalling the events leading up to the crime. He described being chased through a large marble hall by a swarthy-faced man in white robes who caught him and forced him to swallow a liquid from a glass vial. It was not merely a series of images but a reliving of a distressing experience. He once again felt the fear of being caught, then felt his throat tighten from the effects of the poison.

Seeing how upsetting it was for his client the therapist interjected, encouraging him to move on.

'Take yourself back to the death experience,' he suggested, at which Tony found himself released from the lifeless body and looking down on it with detachment.

Then he was asked to move forward.

> *There was a shimmering pearl-like light all around me and I was weightless, free, floating in the sky. Then I entered a dazzling light and there was an Egyptian woman waiting there who came to me, her arms open. Her hair was plaited in magnificent braids and she had rings on her fingers and toes and was wearing a pure white tunic that dazzled my eyes. 'Mother,' I remember greeting her, but she wasn't the mother I have now in this life. She was my mother then, and I was somehow completely aware that she had died when I was a baby and that she now had her arms outstretched. 'Come,' she said, and totally unafraid I went to her. She then took me by the hand and led me away… This is how I know what it is like to die.*

Stockwell was dancing with a female friend at a party when he had a spontaneous vision of the two of them dancing in the 1920s

In contrast Tony's last life was far more mundane. If his recollections are to be relied upon he was a music hall entertainer in the British coastal town of Bournemouth just prior to the First World War. These images of the past had been haunting him since his childhood and were consistent, a fact which convinced him that they were not a product of his imagination. They took the form of spontaneous flashbacks in which he saw himself as a handsome young man of about twenty with slicked-back, Brylcreemed hair. He was entertaining the holiday crowds on the pier and taking tea from a blue-and-white striped pot in a local café.

Even though Tony had no doubt in his mind that the flashbacks were genuine he was delighted when it was confirmed during a recent visit to the town. On a stroll through the streets he predicted he would find the café round a corner, which he proceeded to do although he had never been to Bournemouth before in his present lifetime.

Some months later he was dancing with a female friend at a party when he had another spontaneous vision of the two of them dancing in the 1920s. His partner looked the same but her name then was Daphne and his was Archie. Tony had always suspected that he had known his really close friends in a past life and this flashback appeared to confirm it.

When asked by friends how he can be sure that these visions are genuine he replies that while dreams are merely random and often nonsensical, these flashbacks involve all the senses. He is not merely recalling a repressed memory, he is experiencing that incident from a former life all over again.

Psychic Agony Aunt

A LESSER-KNOWN but no less remarkable medium is Jill Nash, an indomitably cheerful English lady whose down-to-earth approach to the paranormal must qualify her as the psychic Miss Marple.

She experienced her first spontaneous glimpse into a past life during a day trip to Arundel Castle in Sussex many years ago:

Although I had never been there before I immediately felt as if I had

Jill Nash had her first glimpse into a past life on a visit to Arundel Castle. She saw medieval ladies in tall hats with veils and long sleeves

come home. Our guide couldn't remember the shortest way to the castle, but I was able to lead the entire coach party along the right paths as if I was retracing my steps from centuries before. When I entered the Great Hall I went into a kind of dream state in which I saw medieval ladies in tall pointed hats with veils and long sleeves, not as ghosts but as glimpses into the past, as if they were part of the fabric of the building. I wasn't frightened, but excited. I felt that I belonged, but I also had the strongest feeling that my life there had been short. It wasn't a profound or life-transforming experience, but it was enough to confirm my beliefs in

> *reincarnation and it also explained my lifelong fascination with tapestries which I have been able to make without ever having been taught.*

A similar incident occurred in 1996 when she went on holiday to Egypt:

> *As the tour guide was explaining their customs and culture I turned to my husband and said quietly, 'It was different in ancient times,' and described what I intuitively knew to be the way they lived. A moment later the guide said, 'Of course in the days of the pharaohs they did X, Y and Z,' and repeated the details of the scene I had just described.*
>
> *The same happened when we visited the ruins of the temple of Isis at Karnak. As the guide was describing the way the interior looked at the time of the pharaohs I turned to my husband and described*

On a holiday to Egypt in 1996, Jill found she was familiar with her surroundings, but there was unfinished business

'I remember seeing something curious at the end of my bed. It was a beautiful, bright, pulsating, strong white light'

the scene in detail with the hanging silk drapes and other details which the guide didn't comment upon until later.

But the longer we stayed at the site the more oppressive the atmosphere became until I was overcome and suffered an epileptic fit. I had obviously felt the need to return to that place to find some sort of closure, as the bereavement counsellors call it, but it just brought back the emotional distress. I'm now convinced that I had been a handmaiden and was killed by a man with a cobra armband for defending my mistress. The method of murder for women at that time was death from the bite of a poisonous snake and that, I am absolutely certain, accounts for my fear of snakes.

On another occasion I went to a lecture on Elizabethan England and afterwards I asked the speaker if it was true that they had used lavender to clean their clothes in those days. Although I didn't have any specific recollection of a former life in that period I remembered a lot of small but significant domestic details which he was able to confirm. He was very impressed and said, 'I see that you've studied the subject.' Of course I hadn't, but I had to pretend that I had because he probably wouldn't have believed me if I told him how I knew.

Since childhood Jill has instinctively known that the material world is not the only reality; that there are other levels of existence which we are not conscious of but which we can perceive with the sixth sense of psychic sensitivity. But it was not until she was sixteen that she had confirmation of this in a way that left no room for doubt.

I was hospitalized with viral pneumonia, a very serious illness. The doctors doubted that I would pull through so they sent for my mother and father and told them that I was at a critical point in the illness.

After they'd gone I remember lying in bed and seeing something curious at the end of my bed. It was a beautiful, bright, pulsating, strong white light. I couldn't see anything in the light but I had the strongest sense that there was a presence in the middle of it which was communicating with me.

In my mind I could hear it say, 'We are not ready for you yet. You still have a lot to do in this life.' That was the first time I had confirmation that there is a next step after this life, here on earth. I wasn't afraid at all. I was calm, relaxed and peaceful. It was a reassuring presence and I wanted to go to it because I had been very ill and I knew that by entering the light the sickness and anxiety would be taken away. I can't describe what was in the light but I felt it was an all-embracing energy, a lot of unconditional love and understanding.

I must have drifted off to sleep then because the next thing I knew I was awake, the fever had gone and I was inclined to dismiss the experience as a dream or something I had imagined, brought on by the illness or medication. And in a sense it was imagination because we can only perceive another reality and higher frequencies or vibrations of energy through our sixth and more acute sense which we call our imagination.

Unfortunately I couldn't tell my parents because they were strict Methodists and sneered at any form of psychic phenomena. Frankly, I think they were frightened of anything which challenged their faith. It made them uncomfortable. I used to sense a presence occasionally and my mother would shut me up by shouting, 'I don't want to hear about dead people.' But I was never scared because I know nothing really dies. Energy can't die. It can only be transformed.

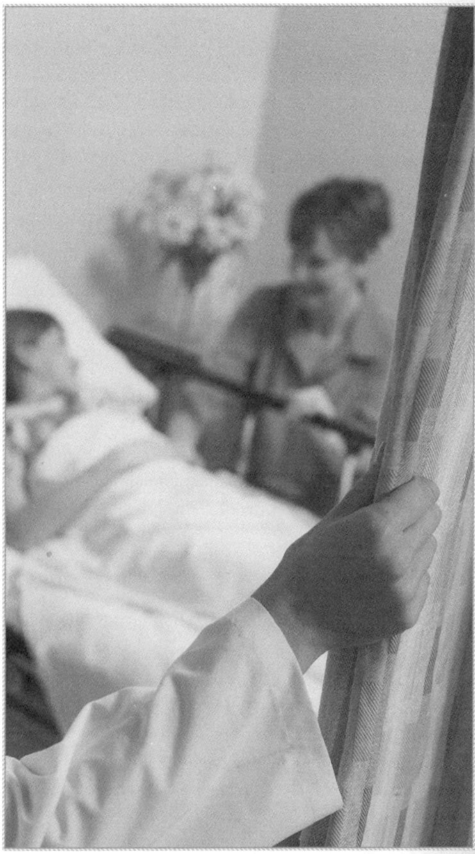

Jill Nash was hospitalized with viral pneumonia and the doctors doubted she would pull through, so they sent for her mother and father

Jill discovered the truth of the saying 'For those who believe no proof is necessary and for those who do not believe, no proof is enough' when she gave a reading to a hardened sceptic:

I was offering past life readings at a psychic fayre when I was approached by a man who challenged me to prove that there is life after death by showing him who he had been in a previous life.

He said, 'If you can tell me exactly what I was told a few weeks ago by someone else then I might believe in life after death.'

I wasn't going to be bullied so I silently asked for help from my friends up there, my guides in spirit, and I immediately felt as if I was being flown backwards on a flying carpet. That's the sensation I have when I connect with someone's past life. I saw this man as he had been in an earlier century. He was a Turkish merchant haggling in a bazaar. He looked different to the way he does in this life but it was him. It was the same personality in a different body. When I described what I was seeing

Jill Nash had a vision of the man as he had once been, a Turkish merchant haggling in a bazaar. It was the same personality in a different body

he was absolutely gobsmacked as that was exactly what he had been told by someone else who had given him a reading. He staggered out as if he had been bopped between the eyes.

Another time I gave a reading to an elderly man who I sensed carried a great burden with him from life to life. As I held his hands to make the connection I saw in my mind a scene of him and a woman as they had been in an earlier incarnation and then again as they are now. I told him that there was a recurring, unresolved conflict between the two of them and that the source of this problem was a disagreement over property, just as it had been in a previous life. She had followed him through from life to life because she had felt cheated and wanted him to make amends.

When I had finished the reading he told me that I had just described his ex-wife and that their relationship had been dominated by a disagreement over their property and that he had always suspected that her resentment and distrust were so strong that it must have originated in a past life because the present quarrel hadn't merited such strong feelings. So that shows what can happen when you can't let go of something or somebody. You bind yourself to them and by doing so hold back your own progress.

Jill's cheerful disposition and pragmatic approach to the subject of past lives was severely tested on one memorable occasion:

Several years ago I went to what is known in psychic circles as a 'fledgling evening', which is the name given to a meeting of people who wish to develop their psychic gifts under the guidance of an experienced teacher. On this occasion the group was being led by a highly regarded Jungian psychologist and qualified counsellor called Nanette Philips.

I didn't know Ms Philips at that time, but I had a nagging suspicion that I had seen her somewhere before as soon as I entered the room. In fact, the feeling became so strong I had to ask if we had met before. She said we hadn't but then asked me to close my eyes, relax and describe what I felt or saw. I felt a bit awkward doing that with everyone looking at me, but I did as she asked and was soon overcome by a tingling and terrific heat all over my body. That was strange because we were in a chilly hall in the middle of winter. The heat became so intense that I began to sweat.

It was then that I saw images of ancient Egypt and saw myself in a vast temple. Ms Philips was there too, but not as she is now. She was dressed as a priestess of Isis and was cowering behind me as a large, imposing man approached. I lost all sense of where I was physically and was literally transported back in time.

I described aloud to the group what I was seeing and as soon as I mentioned the man I heard Ms Philips take a sharp intake of breath. He was stern and very, very threatening. He was

covered from head to foot in red ochre body paint and wore a short pleated skirt-type dress and a gold arm band embossed with a cobra. A thick scar ran from his right wrist to his elbow and part of his left ear was missing. It seemed to me as though he had come to take her to be killed for something she had done or been accused of doing. She was to be put to death by the bite of a poisonous snake – the thought of which gave me a shiver as I have always had an irrational fear of snakes and this might explain why. The man wasn't after me, but I was still terrified. It became so bad that I had to come out of it, shaken and exhausted.

It was then that Ms Philips revealed that she had recently been to a regression therapist and everything I had described she herself had seen during that session. Moreover, the session had been recorded and she promised to bring the tape in the next day for our second meeting so that we could all hear that what I had seen and experienced had been shared by the two of us. But that wasn't the end of it. The following day I went to the local library to see if I could find any books about ancient Egypt to shed some light on what I had seen and on the inner flap of the dust jacket of the first book I picked up there was a photo of the very same gold arm band that I had seen complete with the serpent symbol. Since that day I no longer believe in coincidence.

Psychic healer Karin Page begins a past life reading by examining the subject's aura, the radiance of etheric energy surrounding the body

Images in The Aura

GERMAN-BORN PSYCHIC healer Karin Page is the guiding force behind The Star of The East spiritualist centre in Kent which trains healers and holds fledgling meetings to encourage members to develop their psychic sensitivity in the safety of a supervised circle. She describes what she sees and senses when giving a past life reading.

I begin by looking into their aura, the radiance of etheric energy surrounding the body. Often I will see scenes from their former lives as vivid impressions as if I was sharing their memories, or a guide may appear and lead me into a flashback from their former life. Even though the features of my client will be different, their personality and physical characteristics will be strikingly similar.

Frequently I will see a transfiguration as the face of their former self is superimposed on their present features. It is nearly always a significant scene, rarely a mundane or routine incident, and even if its significance is lost to me the client will say, 'Now I understand why such and such has been happening to me,' or 'That explains why I have had a lifelong fear of something.'

Karin is a firm believer in not asking others to do what she has not tried and tested for herself.

> *I used to suffer from intense migraines until a regression session revealed the source of my headaches. I learnt that I had a life in Scandinavia as the young wife of an uncouth publican in which my only pleasure had been horse riding. Under hypnosis I saw myself riding this beautiful white horse and felt the exhilaration and freedom that I had enjoyed at that time. Then the horse shied and I fell, striking my head on one of the kegs of ale in the yard and died from a fatal head injury. After that session I never suffered from migraines again.*
>
> *Regression has also helped me to discover my karmic connection to other people and why I feel the need to look out for them in this life. I have even learnt why I have a compulsion to keep a full larder of food. It appears that I had a life as an impoverished Indian girl who was hanged by a mob for stealing food for her seven starving brothers and sisters. Curiously, when I was born in my present incarnation the umbilical cord wrapped itself around my neck and I was suffocated. The doctors managed to revive me, but for years afterwards I had this strangulation scar around my neck.*
>
> *Another time I was regressed to a life as a novice monk in medieval Cologne where I died in a fire and witnessed the abbot's vain attempt to rescue me. I immediately recognized him as someone I knew in my present incarnation and later learnt that my friend had been told independently by a clairvoyant that he had a former life as an abbot in Cologne. It was the confirmation I needed, although when you re-experience a past life you know intuitively at the core of your being if it is true or not. I don't need a scientist's approval to convince me of the validity of my experience.*

Karin had always felt an affinity for John, a close friend and a tireless charity worker, who delivered emergency supplies to disaster areas around the world, often at considerable risk to his own life.

Despite his arduous and demanding schedule he always seemed to turn up when she needed advice, so often in fact that she suspected there must be a karmic link between them. During a regression session she recalled a previous life in which she had been his sister and had drowned herself after being abused by her employer. John had been unable to save her, but had vowed to be there for her in the next life whenever she needed him.

But the most affecting regression experience she had was that which revealed a previously unknown link to celebrated psychic surgeon Stephen Turoff, whose miraculous healing powers are said to be the result of his possession by spirit guide Dr Kahn, who had been a physician in nineteenth-century Vienna:

I went to Stephen for treatment many years ago. He was then working in trance. He allowed Dr Kahn to guide his hands and speak through him. The physical transformation from the gentle six foot giant to wizened physician was striking. Through Stephen, Dr Kahn told me that he had been looking after me since I was a child and that I would understand the significance of what he said very soon.

I later learnt during meditation of a former life in Vienna as the wife of a poor medical student who had tried to deliver our baby at home by himself. But I died in childbirth and as I died I saw him on his knees weeping and vowing to become the best doctor in all Europe so that no mother would have to die in childbirth as I had done. He had been the son of Dr Kahn and that baby returned to me in my present life as my own son. So I learnt that nothing and no one is really lost to us. Separation and grief are only temporary. Our love ensures that we meet again.

The Case Against Reincarnation

Where is the evidence that we have evolved? After all these years, we are still a materialistic, violent and largely self-centred species

THE SCEPTIC'S argument against reincarnation centres on two specific points: the lack of scientific evidence proving the existence of the human soul (which this book has hopefully addressed) and the fact that there is no indication that humanity has evolved significantly in the past 2,000 years. In other words, we have apparently not benefited from experiences gleaned from successive lives.

We are still a materialistic, violent and largely self-centred species and not a race of enlightened souls. For every Ghandi there are a hundred tinpot dictators and for every selfless humanitarian there are countless criminals, serial killers, spiteful destructive yobs and mean-spirited individuals who are determined to prove that they are right and everyone else is wrong. And let's be honest, none of us are the compassionate, even-tempered, selfless individuals we would like to be. We are all a mass of contradictions and the prey of mixed emotions. If life is a school, as the mystics would have us believe, then the majority of us are still fighting for the best toys in the sandpit, crying in self-pity when we don't get our own way.

That said, we are beginning to look for the light, to become more self-aware. As more and more people turn away from the rigidity and dogma of organized religion, the interest in spiritual movements and practices such as meditation and other methods of self-realization has grown. And yes, there is a growing threat from fundamentalism and the advocates of Intelligent Design, who stubbornly deny the physical evidence of evolution. But this mob mentality is simply an expression of a fear of the unknown and an unwillingness to change. These reactionaries are, unfortunately, vociferous and capable of slowing down our inexorable progress, but they cannot turn back the clock.

The incredible technological advances made by the human race, coupled with a growing understanding of the universe, are confirmation that the human mind has an infinite potential, whereas history has shown us that the human spirit is indomitable, even in the face of persecution and physical destruction.

Again, the analogy of the growing child is worth making. While some of us are willing to explore the world that surrounds us and the world that is within us, others are resisting this natural development and are seeking security in the familiar because it is the safer option. But if we are afraid to even consider the possibility that this life is not the only one we will experience then we may as well rip up the maps we have made of the universe and go back to believing in a flat earth at the end of which there are dragons waiting to devour the foolhardy traveller. The problem is not human beings but human nature, the primitive lower self or ego which is self-centred, self-serving, self-indulgent and occasionally even self-destructive.

A willingness to accept the possibility of the existence of the human soul and by implication, the law of karma and reincarnation opens the mind to a greater reality and the willingness to learn from experience. Given the choice, which path would you choose?

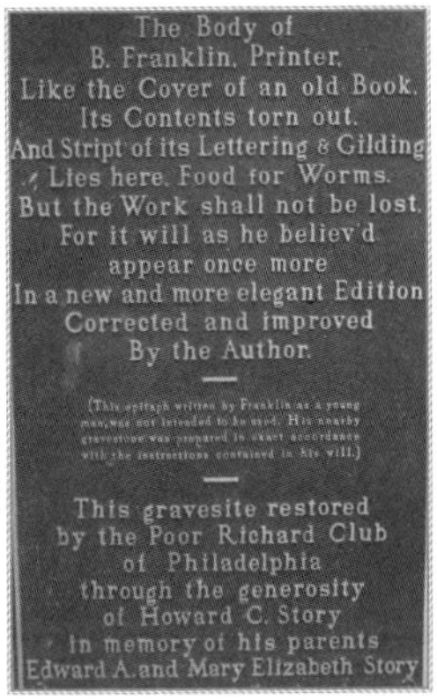

THE BODY OF B. FRANKLIN, PRINTER, LIKE THE COVER OF AN OLD BOOK, ITS CONTENTS TORN OUT AND STRIPPED OF ITS LETTERING AND GILDING, LIES HERE, FOOD FOR WORMS. BUT THE WORK SHALL NOT BE LOST, FOR IT WILL AS HE BELIEVED APPEAR ONCE MORE IN A NEW AND MORE ELEGANT EDITION REVISED AND CORRECTED BY THE AUTHOR.

Epitaph of Benjamin Franklin,
written when he was twenty-one

I look upon death to be as necessary to the constitution as sleep. We shall rise refreshed in the morning.

Benjamin Franklin, aged 88

WHAT IF REINCARNATION IS REAL?

IT IS ONE THING to believe in reincarnation, but quite another to accept it as a fact of life. The majority of the world's population is able to accept the premise and presumably they wouldn't be surprised if one day science was able to prove it beyond any doubt, but it takes a quantum shift in perception to live your present life on the understanding that it is only one in a continuing series of incarnations. If everyone who believed in the possibility of reincarnation actually lived their present life in the certainty of this knowledge and according to the law of karma (cause and effect), the effect on the world and the way we live would be profound.

The first benefit of belief would be that we would lose our fear of death and the pain of bereavement. We would still suffer the wrench of physical separation from our loved ones, but it would be mitigated by the knowledge that we would be reunited with them at some future date on the other side of life. Our obsession with wealth and possessions would cease to have such a hold over us and we would accept that everything in this life is transient. Only our memories, experiences and achievements would have value. That is why whenever someone knows that they are about to die their only thought is for the family they leave behind and the one thing they are determined to do is to reassure those they love of that fact. It would be hard to imagine anyone on the point of death imploring their family to take good care of their plasma TV. In short, our values would change. The result of this reassessment of our true purpose and priorities would be that we would no longer need to reincarnate but would break free of the endless cycle of death and rebirth.

Racial bigotry, religious intolerance, rabid nationalism and even sexual discrimination would all cease at a stroke once the realization had struck home that we have all at one time or another been born into different ethnic backgrounds and have incarnated as both men and women and will doubtless do so again. Rigidity of religious belief would become an anathema to the advanced souls who are able to accept that they might have been devout Muslims, fervent Christians, Orthodox Jews and perhaps even ardent atheists in previous incarnations. In fact, orthodox religion might become redundant when we realize that we are all in essence divine and in no need of a specific doctrine to guide us. That might be why these religions have rejected the doctrine of reincarnation while their esoteric traditions have continued to cherish it as a long-forgotten teaching to be imparted to those seeking the universal truths at the heart of their tradition.

Tribalism in all its forms would be rendered redundant as we lost our fear of those who worship in a different way. There would be no reason for fanatics to impose their beliefs on others. Conflict would fizzle out with no fuel to feed the flames, violence would decrease and crime would be something as alien to our nature as human sacrifice if we accept that our lives are governed by the inviolable universal law of karma, which states that we answer for our actions.

Individuals who feel hard done by, who feel that life is a lottery that has been weighed against them, would stop blaming fate for their misfortunes and instead look to their own attitudes and actions as a possible cause.

The law of karma is often cited as an excuse for not taking responsibility for one's life. In India the 'untouchables' of the lowest caste adhere to the belief that they deserve their lowly status and its attendant hardships because they accrued 'bad karma' in a previous life. But karma is not punishment, it is simply the result of our past actions and it can be reversed by an effort of will. In fact, we incur karmic debt to awaken us to the fact that we are capable of creating our own heaven and hell here on earth. The reality of reincarnation is that it is free will that determines our lives, not Fate.

Unfortunately, few of us are ready to renounce our self-centred way of life and to take responsibility for the world we have made and to which we will one day return. But believers say it is only a matter of time until we do. Then humanity will have taken the next and perhaps final step in its evolution from an aggressive primitive species to the fully realized human beings that it is our potential to become.

If you want to know your past life, look into your present condition; if you want to know your future life, look into your present actions.

Tibetan Buddhist Teaching

✦ Self-Regression ✦

The following exercise can be performed lying down or seated, but if you are lying on a bed or mat remember to support your head with a pillow.

Make yourself comfortable, close your eyes and focus on your breath. With every inhalation repeat the phrase 'calm and centred', and with every exhalation repeat the phrase 'deeply relaxed'.

Do not try to induce an experience. Simply let go and allow yourself to sink into a state of deep relaxation and profound peace as if you were settling into a warm bath.

When you feel suitably relaxed, visualize yourself enveloped in a white mist. It is so dense that you cannot see beyond it. Looking down all you can see is your feet at the top of a flight of steps. The mist clears just enough to reveal that you are standing at the top of a spiral staircase. The lower steps are obscured by the mist. Steady yourself by gripping the handrail to your right and count aloud as you descend.

'One… I am relaxed and ready; two… going down; three… deeper; four… deeper; five… down and round; six… going deeper; seven… deeper down; eight… relaxed and ready; nine… deeper; ten… down.'

You have reached the bottom of the staircase, but still all you can see are your feet and the ground. What type of footwear, if any, are you wearing? What kind of ground are you standing on? The mist begins to clear. You are outside in a landscape that is strangely familiar. Do you recognize this place? Can you tell which country it is from the scenery or the plants? What is the season? Are there any clues as to what period you might be in? What feelings do you associate with this place?

Feel free to explore, knowing that you can return any moment you choose.

Are there any buildings nearby? If so, are you attracted to one in particular? Approach the entrance. Did you live here? Did you work here? If not, what did you do here? Who were your neighbours and what is your abiding memory of this place?

Go inside and look around. Have no fear. No one can harm you. You have returned because there is something of significance for you here. What is it?

Is there a mirror or a basin of water in which you can see your reflection? What clues can you find to your identity? Is it a period when there might be photographs, or a portrait?

If this is a place you knew in a former life you should know what is around the next corner. Test your memory by trying to find specific rooms.

Perhaps there is a skill that you used to practise in a particular room, or a device that you operated? If so, can you locate it and recall how it works?

Perhaps you were a person of importance and this place might hold a clue as to why you feel that you are under-appreciated in your present life. Or perhaps something bad happened here and you left your former life bearing resentment towards someone or guilt for something that you did. If so, do not indulge in these dead emotions. Return with the details so that you can address the issue at a later date, but leave the emotions behind. If there is a basin of water nearby plunge your hands into it and let the residue of your emotional energy dissolve in the water. If not, clutch an object and discharge the negative energy into this.

When you are ready, return to waking consciousness in the usual way. Remember: during a regression there is no need to be anxious. You are in control at all times. If you feel uneasy for any reason, simply return to waking consciousness by counting down from ten to one.

Further Reading

Atwater, P.M.H., *Coming Back To Life*, Ballantine, 1991

Currie, Ian, *Visions Of Immortality*, Element, 1998

Edward, John, *One Last Time*, Penguin Puttnam, 2000

Fremantle, R. and Trungpa, C., *The Tibetan Book Of The Dead*, Shambhala, 1975

Green, Celia, *Out-Of-Body Experiences*, Institute Of Psychophysical Research, 1995

Guirdham, Dr, *The Cathars And Reincarnation*, 1970

Halevi, Shimon Ben, *Kabbalistic Universe*, Gateway, 1988

Head, Joseph and Cranston, S.L., *Reincarnation, The Phoenix Fire Mystery*, Warner, 1979

Holroyd, S., *Mysteries Of The Inner Self*, Aldus, 1978

Jung, C.G., *Memories, Dreams, Reflections*, Vintage Books, 1961

Leland, Kurt, *The Unanswered Question*, Hampton Roads, 2002

MacLaine, Shirley, *Out On A Limb*, Bantam, 1984

Monroe, R.A., *Journeys Out Of The Body*, Doubleday, 1971

Moody, R.A., *Life After Life*, Mockingbird Books, 1975

Moody, R.A., *The Light Beyond*, Rider, 2005

Morse, Melvin, *Closer To The Light*, Ivy Books, 1991

Muldoon, S., *The Case For Astral Projection*, Aries Press, 1936

Muldoon, S., *The Phenomena Of Astral Projection*, Rider, 1987

Myers, F.W.H., *Human Personality And Its Survival Of Bodily Death*, Longmans, Green, 1903

Osis, K. and Haraldsson, E., *At The Hour Of Death*, Hastings House, 1977

Praagh, James Van, *Talking To Heaven*, Signet, 1999

Ring, Kenneth, *Lessons From The Light*, Moment Point Press, 2000

Ring, Kenneth, *Life At Death*, Quill, 1982

Rinpoche, Sogyal, *The Tibetan Book of Living and Dying*, Rider, 2002

Roland, Paul, *The Complete Kabbalah Course*, Foulsham, 2005

Roland, Paul, *Investigating The Unexplained*, Piatkus, 2000

Semkiw, Walter, MD, *Born Again*, Ritana Books, New Delhi, 2006

Various editors, *Mysteries of The Unknown*, Time-Life Books, 1987–91

Zaleski, Carol, *Otherworld Journeys*, Oxford University Press, 1988

Resources

http://www.carolbowman.com

http://www.crystalinks.com/karmasoulgroups.html

http://www.gnostic-jesus.com

http://www.healpastlives.com

http://www.hypnoticworld.co.uk/regression_pastlife

http://www.johnedward.net

http://www.laughingcherub.com/reincarnation.htm

http://www.near-death.com

http://www.nderf.org/

http://iands.org/index.php

http://www.paulroland.net

http://www.pastlives.net

http://www.vanpraagh.com

Index

Picture Credits

Corbis: 7, 10, 33, 35, 38, 48, 51, 60, 65, 66, 70, 71, 72, 78, 88, 95, 104, 112, 114, 116, 125, 128, 133, 134, 136, 142, 143, 146, 150, 151, 152, 154, 162, 171, 176, 178, 180, 182, 183, 186, 192, 197, 201, 202

Mary Evans: 70, 74, 75, 140, 160, 173

Getty Images: 75

Akg images: 130

Bridgeman Art: 92

Science Photo Library: 67, 185, 194

Individual contributors: 11 – Premasagar Rose; 16 – Roland Cervantes Gómez; 17 – Steve Evans; 24 – flickrname:spiralz; 30 – Marianna Koutná; 37 – flickrname: parhessiastes; 42 – Zeynep Kanra; 54 – Dr Arun Rajendran; 81 – Michel Roland-Guil; 110 – flickrname: FT1; 131– flickrname: Bright Meadow; 188 – Mark Tollerman

We have made every attempt to contact the copyright-holders of the photographs and illustrations within this book. Any oversights or omissions will be corrected in future editions.